COPING WITH YOUR EMOTIONS

PAUL J. GELINAS

THE ROSEN PUBLISHING GROUP, Inc.
New York

Published in 1979, 1983, 1989 by The Rosen Publishing Group
29 East 21st Street, New York, N.Y. 10010

Copyright 1979, 1989 by Paul J. Gelinas

Revised Edition 1989

Library of Congress Cataloging in Publication Data

Gelinas, Paul J
  Coping with your emotions.

  Includes index.
  1. Emotions. 2. Developmental psychology.
3. Success. I. Title.
BF561.G44   158'.1   79–1045
ISBN 0–8239–0970–0

Manufactured in the United States of America

About the Author

PAUL J. GELINAS is a clinical psychologist in private practice and a lecturer at the University of the State of New York at Stony Brook. He is a former teacher and superintendent of schools. His educational degrees include the B.A., M.A., M.Sc. and Ed.D.

He is the author of twelve books, two of which were selected as bonus books by the Book-of-the-Month Club.

Among his professional affiliations, he is a member of the Suffolk County Psychological Association and the Council for the Advancement of the Psychological Professions and Sciences. He is listed in such publications as the *National Register of Health Services in Psychology, National Register of Educational Researchers, Contemporary Authors*, the *World Who's Who of Authors*, and the *Dictionary of International Biography*.

His civic activities include positions on the Three Village Board of Education and the Civic Association of the Setaukets, and he is a former president of the Lions Club of Setauket.

As special recognition of his contributions to community leadership, the Paul J. Gelinas Junior High School in Setauket, New York, was named for him.

Contents

CHAPTER I

Aims of Emotional Stability

It is obvious that you can lead a more satisfying life if you know where you are going, if your aims are directed toward worthwhile goals. Many young people lack a vision of purpose, stumbling in a vain search for self-fulfillment without stopping for a moment to take stock of behavior and habits that often seem self-defeating. Others are well adjusted and happy, keeping their equilibrium in the midst of changes and the hazards of modern society.

Understand Your Emotions

Serious emotional difficulties occur when you cannot adjust to your surroundings. Friends are few, there is no challenge in school or work, and a bleakness descends like a pall upon your existence. Somehow things are askew and life seems distorted, with little meaning.

This unhappiness may be attributed to wrong attitudes or poor training, or it may be the result of loss of love, social pressures, and general inability to fit well with other people. Of course, sickness, loss of friends, and many other factors may combine to make a person's life comparatively barren. Perhaps you are living with parents who fail to understand your state of mind. There may be excessive responsibilities coupled with fear of failure.

Everyone at some period of his or her life has a point at which no more can be tolerated. Even a serious failure in handling one's emotions may be unrecognized until an emergency arises. A great disappointment occurs that taxes your personal resources. You may be sadly shaken, admitting inadequacies that you had not hitherto suspected in yourself. Past experiences and habits in the handling of

3

your emotions will determine whether or not you will be able to weather the storm.

Suitable emotions are facilitated by knowing that your every act produces definite consequences. Cause and effect operate in one's emotional life just as surely as they do in the physical world. The wise person learns to analyze his emotions in terms of their causes and their consequences. In other words, you should understand your conduct and that of others. This habit of probing for reasons underlying the things you do will help you to develop an attitude of sympathy rather than of condemnation toward people's actions, an approach that is fundamental to a healthy emotional point of view.

You may not be aware of your own motives or the real reasons why you act in a given way. To achieve emotional maturity, you should understand what motivates your behavior. Why do you behave the way you do? This matter of self-understanding is so important that psychologists often go through psychotherapy themselves in order to appreciate the motives that may unconsciously dominate their lives. Self-understanding is vital before one can presume to help others who seek psychological services.

Self-understanding or the ability to analyze your emotions involves knowing what sort of person you really are and the person you would like to be. This self-evaluation will enable you to judge what progress you are making toward realizing your goals. On the other hand, you may be lost emotionally because you do not know what your aims are. The solution in this instance must be to formulate your goals and then examine what you want to become in terms of steps that you actually take to reach your objectives.

The basic aim is to become a mature person emotionally. This process of change, of growing up emotionally at any age, is not easy; it requires considerable effort, but it is a creative endeavor with your own happiness as the ultimate goal. Speaking of emotional maturity does not imply that a specific pattern must be followed by everybody. It is not a call for conformity. The aim should be improvement, not perfection. The goal should be uniquely yours. However, we can enunciate certain basic principles. An emotionally mature person will have some or all the following characteristics:

1. Independence
2. Sociability
3. Self-esteem
4. Ability to face reality
5. Balanced life
6. Integration
7. Scale of values

Let us consider each of these characteristics in greater detail.

Independence

The mature person has lessened the emotional dependence on parents. In contrast to your childhood days when you felt more or less tied to the moods and demands of your mother and father, you can now adopt a less dependent relationship to these authority figures. You will feel more like a person in your own right, making up your own mind. This does not mean that you must openly rebel, nor must you ignore other people's suggestions or opinions. You give these their proper regard without feeling that you are compelled to deny ideas that are not worthy of your consideration. This is not defiance of parental authority; it expresses an inner confidence and a trust in your own judgment.

As an adult you are not a "yes" person, overly dependent on other people's decisions for your guidance. You can even be indifferent to social pressures that others feel compelled to follow. You stand on your own feet, not necessarily separated from popular trends—but not a slave to them.

Sometimes normal young people simply refuse to give up their individuality to parents who are perhaps demanding too much. Some parents set impossible goals for their children because of their own sense of insecurity, their inability within their own lifetime to reach a level of achievement that they admire. A mother may be afraid of other people's opinion because of her daughter's behavior. She may be more concerned about a neighbor's remarks than she is about her daughter's welfare. The father may be worried because of his son's lack of discipline. Each parent is striving desperately to maintain self-respect by seeking to mold his adolescent child into his own likeness or that which he deems good.

Wise parents are more concerned with a healthy personality in their children than with school achievement or success on the job. Parents who have their children's best interests at heart will strive to have them develop individuality, to make them feel secure and wanted.

If you have been lucky enough to have had good parents, there need be little worry about your future. You can feel confident that somehow you will make your way in a manner that will prove satisfactory to both you and your parents. Again, let us emphasize that this does not mean you will automatically reject the guidance of those older than yourself. It mainly indicates that you will weigh their opinions carefully in terms of your own individuality and your welfare.

Sociability

Sociability in this context refers to spontaneity in getting along with others. It is essential to be happy in social relations. You should be able to express affection without embarrassment, expecting that your friendly overtures will be reciprocated. This faith is based on the assumption that most people are friendly. You can approach both young and old without fear or suspicion, acting freely, undaunted by self-consciousness or paralyzing inhibition. Most people want to be liked and appreciated. You meet their need for approval by showing interest and warmth toward them. Of course, these intimate emotional ties, if they are to be enduring, cannot have pure self-promotion as their aim. Your ability to give accompanied by the capacity to receive combine to add joy to your days.

This concept of mutual "give and receive" is particularly important in sexual relationships. In the mating intimacy, happiness requires the acceptance of the lover, with the full realization that one supplements the other emotionally as well as physically.

Social relationships involve sympathetic consideration of fellow humans. The selfish person who thinks only of himself or herself is following a course that must ultimately drive away those whose friendship and love are sought. The emotionally mature person is conscious of the obligations to others.

Accordingly, because of this awareness, you will be inclined to be considerate of people with whom you associate. Your ability to be socially concerned requires that you become aware of group living as important to counteract most people's tendency to think primarily of their own welfare. Social interest can be used to compensate for any shortcoming that you feel in your own personality.

Having stressed independence as one sign of emotional maturity, it is now wise to mention that dependence upon others—when it does not deprive you of your individuality—is equally important. You must accept the fact of interdependence in order to survive in the rush of modern living. This art of balancing independence with interdependence is necessary to weave a workable pattern of living where trust is basic to our very existence. The more our society develops its technology, the greater becomes the need to trust. Compare the necessity to trust others in your grandparents' time with that of today. You would not live very long if you did not trust the red light at a busy intersection. In our highly mechanized civilization, without trust in machines and those who operate them there would be chaos and disaster.

Self-esteem

It is vital from the point of view of emotional stability that you think well of yourself. In fact, it generally seems necessary that you love yourself before you can expect love and respect from others. This emphasizes the fact that self-respect is linked directly with positive social relationships. Thinking positively about yourself is an important factor in emotional maturity. If you have a poor image of yourself, you cannot expect your colleagues to appreciate your weakness and sense of inferiority.

We are, of course, speaking of self-love in a mature way, based upon an accurate self-evaluation. You must be on guard against conceit as a false sense of self-esteem. Conceit and snobbery are based on an overestimation of one's own value. Some people have been led by unwise parents to believe themselves better than their peers. A child who has been twisted in his self-evaluation by doting parents soon finds that classmates are inclined to deflate his inflated self-image. As an adult he may discover the cruelty of the world as it seeks to put a phony in his place. He will find few friends who will cater to his selfishness, but there will be many who will be ready to break his fragile defenses that worked with his parents but prove useless in a broader and less protected environment.

Make a study of your personal assets and weaknesses. You may admit that your appearance has its flaws; you may conclude that your intellectual level is only average, that others dance better than you do. Make a list of your limitations. Only by honestly recognizing your weaknesses can you acquire a basis for careful planning toward self-improvement. However, don't forget to take stock of your strengths and assets. In these dual acknowledgments you will arrive at an evaluation that is neither too high nor too low.

If you run yourself down, you will probably encounter many people ready to agree with you. If, on the other hand, you are puffed up with self-importance, you will find many who are eager to deflate your ego. If you are honest with yourself, characterized by neither conceit nor false modesty, your security will remain firm; you can have a sense of self-esteem without undue self-importance.

Self-knowledge and acceptance of one's self are both necessary for sound emotional health. A realistic evaluation of your own weaknesses and strengths is helpful in assuring good human relations. Indeed, we are all animals with propensities for many of the failings of the animal world. But we are also endowed with the human capacity of idealism. You are certainly fortunate if you can get a real insight into yourself while at the same time developing an ample degree of tolerance for others' faults and limitations. Really being a friend to yourself creates a freedom that radiates a positive aura felt by others as something wholesome and friendly. This cannot happen if you consistently condemn yourself and consequently wonder if others are unaccepting and against you. It has been pointed out by many psychologists that forgiving yourself is as important as forgiving others.

You are emotionally healthy if you are aware of your own worth because you have trained yourself to see yourself as others see you. As a result, you become pleased with yourself. You have rid yourself of self-deception and have through honesty gained an insight into your good qualities.

If self-worth is to be based on merit, then you should have the opportunities for doing something successfully. A sense of achievement is necessary for emotional health. Unfortunately in growing up too many of us have felt a sense of failure because of lack of approval. In school, often only the highly intelligent student is recognized and praised while the run-of-the-mill pupil is made to feel inadequate. Perhaps our schools stress competition too much at the expense of developing the total personality.

With all the insight you can muster, you still must not take yourself too seriously. You must be able to take an occasional kidding. If you cannot bear this sort of indulgence, your peers may find it convenient and tempting to make you the object of their banter. On the other hand, not being oversensitive, you will be able to see humor even against yourself, joining with them in hearty amusement over your own follies. Being emotionally stable, you will have a sufficiently good perspective of yourself to laugh at your own expense.

Facing Reality

If you have been trained as a child to meet reality, you will be able to cope successfully with problems in adult years. This ability demands a courageous confrontation with misfortune, the facing of disappointments in yourself and in the outside world. This self-reliance is based on your inner security and independence.

If as a child you were spoiled and overprotected, you may have been undermined in your morale and character—and now a reevaluation of your attitudes is in order. This early coddling in the name of love or kindness may have encouraged you to flee from reality and seek an escape in self-deception. Instead of trying to solve your problems realistically, you may be inclined to blame others for your own shortcomings, thus giving up the opportunity for self-improvement. If you deny your limitations too long, the chances are that you may become a chronic worrier. You will demonstrate that your character lacks maturity because you cannot meet your social obligations.

Many people are guided by their hopes and fears, swayed by an inaccurate notion of reality. They may be overoptimistic at times, then overpessimistic. They are unhappy because of their inability to cope with reality.

If you are realistic, you'll face the truth even when it hurts your feelings. Many disturbing situations affect your life and those of your loved ones, and this fact must be anticipated if you are to achieve emotional strength. As the years go by you will encounter severe disappointments, sorrows, and shocks. You may develop a stoic philosophy, becoming hardened to possible disasters, shutting off your emotions in resignation. However, such an outlook on life not only saves you from being hurt, but it also robs you of love and many other emotions that make life worthwhile. Accordingly, you should accept difficulties as challenges to be used, as means of further emotional growth. Courage will be your helpmate, preparing you to fight firmly when hardship strikes. Either you must struggle to avert tragedy or seek to change defeat into success.

An attitude that views adversity as a means of strengthening character will enable you not only to bear up under strain but also to overcome in the process. Such an attitude should not be interpreted as a giving up or a resignation. Certainly, a time will come when it seems wise to adapt yourself to a given situation or demand. However, there are occasions when it would be wiser for you to modify your behavior in accordance with your wishes and what you deem best for your welfare.

A Balanced Way of Life

The term *balance* refers to a breadth of varied interests. Your being is enriched with work, play, and love, budgeted to expend your energy wisely.

If, for example, you devote all your strength to study or work, you are missing out on the enrichment that a variety of satisfactions can bring. A balanced way of life meets both intellectual and physical needs.

Those who specialize too narrowly as a pattern of living restrict their interests and activities. Without variety, these people tend to be unhappy, feeling vaguely that something is missing. Sometimes people of limited outlook do not realize the source of their frustration until they find the strain too severe to tolerate. These people may have established a sort of security in their ruts. Because habits are so persistent, they often experience sharp difficulties in extricating themselves. Older workers who have such attitudes may find themselves very disturbed when they retire.

Putting Things Together

You will become an emotionally mature person if you can organize the various inconsistencies of your nature into a unified personality. Ideally, harmony must exist not only in your own life but also among citizens of the community. Unification is basic to your personal happiness.

Peace of mind depends on your capacity to tolerate mental conflicts. As you grow more mature emotionally, you will train yourself to withstand conflicts that are unavoidable.

Emotional disturbance involves the inability to get things together; the personality is not integrated. The emotionally sick person has a need to be whole again. A healthy person is emotionally sincere. He has a positive image of himself and is able to achieve in productive activities. The well-integrated person can concentrate on a given task and has the capacity to mobilize his talents to best advantage.

It is possible, however, to be too integrated, as exemplified by a person who is so established that he cannot be flexible. If your behavior is varied and adapted to changing conditions, you will be acting wisely according to your own needs. You will have learned that it is not to your advantage to sacrifice adaptability in order to maintain stability. Real integration of personality, you should conclude, demands that you react according to circumstances.

You might conclude that a criminal may be well integrated, leading his life according to unacceptable values. Such a person may seem satisfied in his career. But ultimately we must conclude that an emotionally mature person devotes his endeavors to socially useful activities and ends.

Your Values

If your personality is integrated, you will practice evaluation and discrimination. When confronted with a problem, as a thoughtful and intelligent person you can carefully consider possible courses of action, then imagine the consequences of your action. Fully aware of the complexities of a given situation, you will not oversimplify action by concluding that everything is all good or all bad. You will rather evaluate realistically, judging in terms of degrees of importance, and consequently finding some values more appropriate than others. Having established a practical approach to problems, you will be able to discriminate between trivialities and important matters.

It can be assumed that your goal is a happy life. You will naturally have a better chance of achieving happiness if you use constructive intelligence instead of impulsive behavior. Thrills are not always in your best interests. Your decision should effect long-term satisfaction rather than temporary "highs." Your happiness ultimately is closely tied to the happiness of others. Nevertheless, despite a measure of dependence on other people, emotional health requires that you anchor your happiness on yourself. Some degree of standing on your own feet is necessary for your security.

If you have emotional stability, you will avoid resentment of misfortune and realize the uselessness of self-pity, the destructiveness of nursing a grudge. When circumstances are not satisfactory, you will try to find out whether you are somewhat responsible. Even self-sacrifice will be deemed improper unless it is not purely for personal gain. By linking your activities and goals to those of others, you will strengthen your own personality.

In choosing your work, a sense of belonging and worthwhile achievement should be more significant than income. A feeling that you are doing well with some of your skills will give you a sense of fulfillment.

With a scale of values that you consider valid, you can have your own beliefs and live accordingly. You may be skeptical on occasion, but that will not stop you. If within you there is emotional health you will realize that the world is basically good, that your existence is worthwhile, that there is order in the universe, and that nature can heighten happiness if we work with it and seek to cooperate with it to improve our lot.

With that scale of values that enables you to function constructively with yourself and others, you will have achieved self-respect and a feeling of self-worth. You will then be strong and wise enough to attain the fulfillment of your desires and your happiness.

You will also have learned that you cannot function in a vacuum, that you need other people in order to gain that sense of contentment and happiness sought by any human being.

The study of your emotions is therefore concerned not only with yourself, but also with your interpersonal relationships, your influence on others, and their effects on you.

Incidentally, it should be noted that throughout this book the masculine pronouns and sometimes the noun "man" are used for succinctness and are intended to refer to both sexes.

CHAPTER II

Healthy or Unhealthy Emotions

Approximately 90 percent of the population of the United States are considered normal in the sense that they do not become candidates for a mental institution during their lifetimes. However, most people in the normal category can learn about the effectiveness of their life-style by comparing it with those whose pattern of life makes them obviously abnormal. The characteristics of the emotionally mature person have been examined in the previous chapter. Now the traits of the neurotic person will be considered. It must be emphasized, however, that many characteristics apply to both the so-called normal human being and the person deemed to be abnormal. It was discovered in a New York City study, for example, that about 80 percent of those surveyed indicated that at some time in their lives they could have been in need of psychotherapy.

The assumption that an insane person can be easily distinguished from the normal man or woman is erroneous. The difference between the two is essentially a matter of degree. It has been said that the insane are only a bit crazier than the rest of us. The lunatic in fact displays the hangups that may exist in most of us. Reading a book on abnormal psychology, you may discover that many of the peculiarities noted in a severely disturbed person also exist in a moderate degree in your own personality and among your acquaintances. When speaking of insanity we are referring to exaggerated and consistently irrational behavior. The oddities of the abnormal have to be extreme in order to be considered a serious deviation.

Abnormality of behavior is not fixed and definite. We cannot draw an arbitrary line between the sane and the insane. We may, however, accept as tentative guidelines the fact that people are often hospitalized when characterized by some or all of the following conditions:

1. Bizarre behavior—hearing nonexistent voices, talking to themselves, having odd manners, and making inappropriate remarks that are embarrassing to others.
2. Disorientation—exaggerated tendencies such as throwing away money, attempting suicide, or self-mutilation.
3. Threat to the safety of others—indiscriminate attacks against innocent persons, ruthless destruction of property, or repeated commission of sexual crimes.

Another factor in differentiating the abnormal from the normal is behavior considered appropriate for a given age. What is expected of a very young child differs from that of a grown person. An 18-year-old woman is not generally limited to baby talk.

Strangely, sex enters the picture in this differentiation. A man's extramarital promiscuity is looked upon with greater toleration than that of a woman. The female alcoholic is frequently viewed as more abnormal than the male drunkard.

The dominant culture and prevailing opinion at a given time often determine what is considered normal or its opposite. Certain sexual behavior was accepted as normal in ancient Greece, whereas it is deemed abnormal in our society. Some primitive tribes considered cheating praiseworthy, whereas we condemn it. Certainly the Western system of competition and capitalism is unacceptable in a communistic society.

Normality and abnormality, therefore, are relative terms. People are now inclined to a more wholesome attitude toward the mentally ill. They tend to look on serious emotional disturbances as comparable to physical sickness, with no disgrace involved. Some people still feel ill at ease if they need to visit a psychologist. This is evidence that we need additional education on the nature of mental disturbances. More enlightened people, on the other hand, may accept the fact that they need to grow emotionally by seeking psychoanalysis or other forms of psychotherapy as a means of reaching that goal. After all, the way to avoid self-deception is to gain more self-knowledge. If our aim is happiness, a healthy mind is certainly of vital importance.

The Emotionally Disturbed

If you are emotionally immature, you act in such a way as to assure failure. Your conduct is self-defeating. Your unhappiness is guaranteed by following certain practices that lead to maladjustment. You evade responsibility, giving all kinds of excuses. You lack self-confidence, carry grudges, and are always ready to accuse others, while riddled with self-pity. You may resort to all kinds of tricks to get your own way, frequently avoiding others to maintain your shaky self-esteem. You may have a concept of yourself far in excess of reality. If you are a neurotic person, you are dissatisfied, hopeless, and also destructive and vindictive.

In order to further consider the emotionally disturbed or neurotic person, let us look at some specific characteristics.

Undue Physical Preoccupation

Not all people who talk about their physical illnesses are necessarily neurotic, and as noted earlier there are some similarities between average persons and the emotionally disturbed. It must be re-emphasized that the difference between the average person and the mentally ill is merely a matter of degree. Nevertheless we must realize that neurotics are often overly preoccupied with their physical sicknesses or imagined bodily deficiencies.

Some emotionally unstable persons are eager to share their troubles. They are constant complainers. Their endless claims of suffering and woe are means of competing with others to gain attention. The typical hypochondriac, a person who imagines illnesses, is in his element when describing them to friends and acquaintances. Others may listen for a while, but ultimately they become bored with Mary's recitals of her troubles, perhaps coming to suspect that she glories in them.

The kind of person you are, your ability to meet your own needs through good fellowship, sincerity, and concern for others are the essence of being liked and respected. You are too busy living, enjoying life and friendships to worry about physical deficiencies, which after all are the lot of most people in one way or another. In fact, the famous psychologist Alfred Adler based his system partially on the fact that our limitations are often the main stepping-stone to greatness. Think of the men and women who left their mark on the world. Who could have been uglier than Socrates? You may be proud of your personal appearance, and certainly you should be. But even your own observation among your fellows should show that looks in themselves are not enough. Forget about any inadequacies; rather examine your assets and draw compound interest from your good qualities.

I Want—I Don't Want Syndrome

The neurotic frequently cannot make up his mind. He wants something, and yet he does not want it. His desires are repeatedly in conflict. First he longs for a wished object, then somehow obstacles are mounted in his mind against the wanted object. He wants to practice a given profession but dreads the years of study involved. Marriage may be his goal, but he believes the expected fidelity would be too much for him—and anyway he is sure that her parents would take advantage of him.

Such a person is generally afraid of failure. Undertaking a progressive step involves the possibility of a threat and a demonstration of his inadequacies.

If you are inclined to be indecisive, not able to stick to a course of action, vacillating from one goal to another, perhaps you should build up your sense of security. Begin with small tasks that are easily within your reach, thus augmenting your feeling of achievement. You can then proceed to more difficult situations that will finally be handled with greater ease.

Feelings of Inferiority

Young people with drug or alcohol problems generally have a low opinion of themselves. The aim of "getting high" is often an attempt to get away from their real selves, substituting a crutch against the feeling of inadequacy. The neurotic is dominated by this feeling. He is not equal to the demands of his existence because of a deep-seated inferiority complex.

Such a person may seek to compensate for his shortcomings and unsteady emotions by trying to pose as better than others. He attempts to put them down, to dominate them. He has a compulsive urge to make money as a goal in itself, to excel as a means of showing off. In fact, many people who are nakedly greedy, ruthlessly aggressive, and ambitious are neurotics who are trying to hide their sense of inferiority.

Set your own goals realistically, not to impress others, but rather to satisfy your own needs and those of others in a sincere reflection of your basic personality. Although income may be a factor in your happiness, nevertheless an unhappy millionaire is not to be envied in comparison with the well-adjusted person who is happy in his work and in his capacity to love.

Immediate Pleasure

The emotionally unstable person wants to satisfy his desires immediately. He cannot sacrifice the present for a greater pleasure at a later time. It is characteristic of him to feel that his wish must be realized right now. Like a spoiled child, he sulks and becomes angry if parents, teachers, and peers refuse to cater to his every whim. Frequently rebuffed in his demands for self-indulgence, he promptly displays antisocial attitudes. The world is a lousy place, the enemy is everywhere, society is a selfish monster.

Unlike the person who is realistically aware of injustices but nevertheless is hoping and trying to shape his environment nearer to the satisfaction of other sincere people, the neurotic is not really concerned with improvement in society. He is rather more interested in displaying his anger because his selfish and unreasonable demands are not immediately satisfied. He has little concern for his fellowmen; he merely wants instant gratification without the necessity of waiting until he has made his contribution through socially desirable work toward his own self-improvement and that of others.

If you are to reap lasting satisfaction, you may have to postpone some pleasures from the present to the future. This means sacrificing now in order to achieve the goal of a happy and fulfilling future; it means taking the time, making efforts toward personality improvement and the emotional health that can be yours.

Touchiness

A neurotic goes around with "a chip on his shoulder." Because of his sense of inferiority, he is oversensitive to the possibility that others will underestimate his worth. Keyed up to anticipating degradation, he readily expects insults. His shaky ego leads him to misinterpret a passing comment that was not intended to be derogatory. A young man on a date may comment that the girl would look very attractive with short hair. She immediately interprets the remark to mean that she looks ugly with her present hairdo.

You can doubtless add many other incidents of touchy persons who are ever on the lookout for possible insults, ever on the alert for attacks on their frail personalities. Yet you are somewhat puzzled by the neurotic people who also proclaim that they do not care what others think of them. An oversensitive girl may toss her head insisting that she doesn't give a damn what others may do or say; but you are struck by the vehemence of her assertions, perhaps knowing that she thus betrays the insecurity that may be her constant companion.

The neurotic has generally built up an inflated concept of himself. Deep within him, there exists a brooding sense of inadequacy. He seeks to counter this feeling by creating a false self in his imagination. The resulting vanity attempts to compensate for the emptiness of his deeper self. Having erected this protective device against his weaknesses, he moves with uncertainty in his daily life, living with a false front that is always susceptible to attack and destruction by those who see through his pretense.

It is true, however, that you must think well of yourself. Understanding that you should have a positive opinion of your self-worth, you will accept your good qualities. But pure vanity is something else.

Fear of Competition

The emotionally unstable person lacks self-confidence. He fears competition because he anticipates failure and subsequent humiliation. He does not dare participate in games because he is afraid to lose. He complains that the cards are stacked against him. "Why try?" he asks. "I can't win—I just don't feel like playing today." His opponents become discouraged. "What is the fun of playing against someone who is already a loser?" Indeed, the emotionally unbalanced person is impelled by a subconscious desire for others to dislike him.

This fear and anticipation of failure sometimes leads to avoidance of an examination as a means of escape from the ordeal. The person is afraid that such examination, either physical or mental, will disclose weaknesses and bring humiliation. Some students actually commit suicide before important tests. Others of varying ages avoid medical examinations because they are certain that these will reveal some terrible disease.

Hypercritical Behavior

The neurotic often disparages others as a means of elevating himself. He puts down other people's accomplishments by calling them petty and unworthy. Or he says the success of others is due to lucky breaks, to family connections, or to political pull. In this manner it is easier to downgrade one's fellows than to compete, to equal or to surpass the progress of one's peers. The neurotic actually believes that lowering others serves to boost his own status. The emotionally poor person finds it easier to sympathize with the suffering of a friend than to praise his success. Women have often been accused of being "catty" about other members of their sex. At times due to competition, this sort of criticism is frequently the result of neurotic trends and a sense of one's own inadequacy.

Greater emotional maturity helps one to give credit where credit is due, to praise a person for a job well done, to comment on a friend's fine appearance, fairness, and excellence. This in no way detracts from one's own comparative values. People have a need to be liked, and the exchange of honest compliments is basic to a true and valued friendship. The neurotic, on the other hand, does not dare to respect another's superiority because his own self-esteem is too insecure.

The Urge to Be Punished

Have you ever met someone who felt guilty when he was having a good time? Somehow this kind of person has been conditioned to feel guilty after having what he wants, to feel that he must pay for his pleasure by doing penance.

Because of this guilt associated with pleasure, a neurotic person may hesitate to spend for frivolity, and his date interprets this as stinginess. In reality, he finds it difficult to have fun if the evening involves money, because by doing so he must sacrifice his security, which is so tightly associated with his self-esteem.

In his love affairs, he is often entangled in hopeless situations. He wants somebody else's girl friend or the wife of another man. Frequently if he succeeds in a dangerous relationship, he anticipates severe punishment. He must pay for his action, he believes, and almost welcomes it to propitiate his conscience.

Neurotic parents worry over their children and sometimes overprotect them instead of enjoying them. Yet somehow a sense of tragedy seems ever present. Disaster hovers in the back of their minds as almost inevitable. A child may be struck by a car or maltreated by teacher and peers. Neurotic parents are slaves of their worries, and guilt haunts their thoughts.

The sadness of the neurotic's way of life is that he cannot get any pleasure out of life. He cannot enjoy his work, sex, or play, being in an almost constant state of frustration. Even if great achievement and goals are attained, the emptiness remains. Contentment is beyond realization. His personality makes satisfaction beyond his reach. Peace of mind is always elusive. Worldly goods, position, or even fame turn out to be meaningless because the problems exist within himself, and he cannot overcome these shortcomings without a revaluation of his whole existence.

Not Getting Along With Others

Lack of ability to have meaningful social relationships is a trait of the neurotic person. Self-centeredness, selfishness, and lack of interest in social life combine to isolate him from others, leaving him lonely and sometimes an outcast. Afraid of becoming dependent, he cannot give of himself. Emotional attachment thus becomes a threat to his autonomy. He fears to be in the power of others, feeling that "belonging to others" is tantamount to loss of self-control. This inability to feel himself a part of the community, to assume responsibilities as part of social life, brands him as a social misfit.

Psychologists point out that a neurotic seeks safety above all else because of his basic anxiety. The normal person seeks to move toward people, establishing friendship and a readiness to accept others. The emotionally unstable person, on the other hand, uses others to sustain his shaky ideas of himself. His self-image is so meager that he tends to overestimate the opinions of others. His tendency to possessiveness is due to a fear of being abandoned, deserted—a fate that his personality seems to invite with self-defeating behavior.

The emotionally disturbed person tends to move away from people as a general rule. This takes the form of keeping away from emotional attachments as an impulsive reaction, as an end in itself. The aim is not to be obligated to anyone.

The neurotic's fear of others' motives often leads to hostility against people. Such a person is in constant conflict with his social surroundings, which in turn incapacitates him with hesitancy, envy, and finally discouragement. As a complement, there is a tendency toward destructiveness, an urge to exploit people, and an unreasonable need for power. Rivalry replaces friendly feelings. In the end the neurotic considers himself rejected and surrounded by a hostile world.

Reaching Too High

The person who is afflicted with neurotic trends is usually a perfectionist. In the unrelenting desire to prove his own superiority, he feels that he must always be right, refusing to admit that he has faults or that he might be wrong on occasion. There is a wide discrepancy between what he desires and his actual achievements. His goals are unrealistic and in fact are largely the product of his own imagination. This desire for the impossible is wishful thinking based on fantasies rather than reality. Thus he is bound to be frustrated and angry with his existence. Chasing impractical rainbows takes up so much energy that he has little left for self-improvement and practical accomplishments. Thus having aimed too high must inevitably lead to a sense of failure and loss of self-respect. The normal person carefully weighs his strengths, weaknesses, skills, and faults; the neurotic fails because his aspirations are too high and based on powers that he does not possess.

This does not mean that you should not aim for difficult goals. But if you want to become skilled in some field of endeavor, mere wishful thinking is not enough. The wise person realizes that training, hard work, and devotion are necessary for success, whether it be in work, play, or self-improvement.

Can anything be done for a neurotic person? Here is a brief case history:

Martha was referred to my office by her family physician. She functioned poorly because of a continuous depressive state punctuated by bouts of hostility expressed in a diffused way against parents and associates. At age 19 she had for several years been sexually promiscuous, with little physical or psychological satisfaction.

"All right," she snarled as she sat on the edge of the chair next to my desk. "You're the shrink—my doctor said I should see you; but I'll be damned if I know why I'm here." She fidgeted with her silver bracelet, her eyes hostile.

"Why did you want to see me?" I asked, ignoring the challenge and negativism in her voice.

"I think my doctor's full of shit—there's nothing wrong with me."

"Are you happy? Why are you angry?" Posing the two questions, I awaited her reaction.

She admitted reluctantly, "No, I'm not happy." Then quickly

she regained the attack. "Who the hell *is* happy in this messed-up world?"

"Why not tell me something about yourself," I put in gently, "and then we can decide whether or not you need psychotherapy."

With a sudden and firm toss of her head, her long blonde hair swung to the back of her slim neck, and she looked askance at me as if she were measuring my every move. "I understand that you shrinks charge outlandish fees." She listened with impatience and defiance as I stated my standard fee per session.

"You know," she said bluntly, "I can't afford that much."

In spite of her fashionable and expensive attire, I assumed that she was hard-pressed financially and agreed to lower my fee accordingly. For the first time in the interview, she smiled and giggled slightly with a smug look on her face. She had in fact dominated the situation, and I began to suspect at this point that part of her defense was the need to exploit people.

"I may not be able to pay all at once," she countered with a sort of condition that for the time being seemed to satisfy something within her. It really had nothing to do with money. Three weeks later, tearfully, she broke down and confessed that she could well afford the therapy. "Help me," she said. "I need help—and I'm miserable. I talk big because I hate myself, and I hate you—I hate my mother, my father, too."

"You feel very insecure, and you feel unloved, perhaps even ugly, although you're a beautiful girl."

"Everybody says I'm beautiful; I'm sick of hearing it."

Thus began a long process that lasted more than two years. She was an only child of a prominent lawyer, having ample funds to squander on expensive cars and sudden trips to Europe or Bermuda. She was ever seeking she knew not what nor could she find it—always linked to her need to dominate, to twist people to her own desires as she had so obviously tried to do during her first psychotherapy session. It took some time before she regained a degree of composure with the growth of a sense of security and the realization that she was not a girl against the world and the world against her.

Slowly we had to delve into her early years to find out what had occurred to twist her personality and to determine the factors that now influenced her self-defeating behavior that created more enemies than friends.

Martha's father was hard and ruthless in his profession, apparently viewing the world as a jungle where only the strong could survive. An attractive and clever manipulator of judges and juries, he had as a basic code the belief that others were weak and that words and arguments could exploit their weaknesses in favor of his clients.

The mother accepted her husband's boasting and ranting with endless patience, smiling her little smile, ever taking the part of those weaker and less articulate. Yet in Martha's mind, her mother was spineless and beaten down through the years. She could not identify with her and her seeming submission. So the little girl grew up fearing her father but identifying with him out of that fear, as if it were safer to take his side rather than the more lenient tendency of her fragile and idealistic mother.

Like her father, she sought security by trying to dominate, to maneuver people toward supporting her emotionally—with subsequent defeats, anger, guilt, and finally depression. Her sexual contacts were always contests of will, a desire for control instead of relaxation and love. No matter how many men she attracted, there was always an emptiness because she could not give of herself.

Under the trying psychotherapy sessions, she gradually began to realize the nature of her defenses, reluctantly yielding and accepting the fact that she had been imitating her father, that her mother in her sweet and quiet way was stronger than her father, that she actually controlled the household, understood humanity better than her famous husband.

The transformation of a human personality toward greater self-realization and understanding is a rewarding task for a clinical psychologist or psychiatrist. Martha finally stood on her own feet, having grasped the core of herself. Married to a mild-mannered chemist, she returned to my office with a five-month-old baby girl.

"Are you really happy now—remember I asked that same question more than three years ago?"

She looked at the baby in her arms. "How can you ask such a

foolish question?" she countered. "I don't need you anymore, you money-hungry shrink—remember how I tried to con you into treating me at a lower fee?" She arose and kissed me lightly on the cheek. The receptionist wondered why the woman leaving the office with the baby was laughing with tears at the corners of her eyes.

How to Develop Emotional Strength

Personality is often considered something you are born with. Some people are full of vitality and charm while others are dull and boring. It is true that heredity may be involved, but it is also a fact that anyone can do much to enhance his or her personality. The changes that can be made to improve one's social attractiveness are demonstrated again and again by those who are willing to pay the price of self-improvement. Personality can be acquired and developed. A good mind and a so-called good character are desirable, but even with these a person is handicapped without an effective personality. This can be attained through habits and skills—acquired through practice.

You must stress the value of getting along happily with people. This involves self-discipline, evidenced by a willingness to make an effort. You can at times be ready to subordinate your own impulses and desires to those of your friends and acquaintances. Such a readiness to fill the needs of others does not imply that you are submissive. It merely means that you are secure enough in your own self-image to size up other people's desire to be liked and understood. The emotionally healthy person is used to exerting himself, being active both physically and mentally, utilizing personal energy for greater self-fulfillment.

You can prepare yourself for pleasant human relationships by changing some of the habits that have proven harmful in the past. This statement is based on the assumption that personality is not something that you have, but it is essentially how you act when in the company of others. This is particularly relevant when excessive self-consciousness is a handicap.

Some people are so dominated by self-centeredness that they

cannot let go and be relaxed in groups. The cause of this trouble is, of course, preoccupation with oneself. This bad habit can be neutralized by training, by focusing attention on others.

You will find that nothing wins greater approval, or more enhances your personality, than the habit of being considerate of other people. Thoughtfulness and an awareness of other people's needs contribute not only to the happiness of others, but also to your own. By being aware of those with whom you come in contact, you tend to forget about your own self-consciousness.

The idea that personality is a simple matter of acquiring good habits is particularly pertinent because it emphasizes the fact that you can modify yourself in a way that will bring affection and popularity.

If, therefore, you are not entirely happy with your relationships, you need not resign yourself to a prosaic fate. There is a way out, a door through which you can pass into a new world of more contentment because you will have found a formula. Think of others, express appreciation, note the good points of companions, and as if by magic your own self-consciousness and shyness will be dissipated.

With this new habit, you will soon be known as an attractive person who is inclined to like people, seeing their good qualities. Perhaps you will also note shortcomings in your friends, but you will tend to excuse them in the interest of closer relationships.

The inclination to like a variety of persons does not mean that you must become intimate with those who bore you or who through obnoxious habits tend to be too far out for your own comfort. Certainly, however, the tendency to practice a friendly approach will enrich your circle of friends and increase your sense of belonging.

Unhealthful emotions are often aroused by fears and guilt, but you were not born with those emotions. Someone taught you to be afraid and guilty. Therefore your fears are not your own, and your guilt feelings have similarly been borrowed from someone else. As you mature psychologically, you will realize that these negative emotions are frequently unjustified or grossly exaggerated.

CHAPTER III

Facing the Facts of Life

Emotional health necessitates the ability and readiness to accept reality. The importance of this assumption is emphasized by the fact that one who is mentally ill has either lost touch with the real world or has distorted it beyond recognition. An emotionally stable person is able to evaluate his surroundings in a way that enables him to adjust successfully to life's daily situations. The well-adjusted person lives in a real world. In some instances what he finds may not be to his liking, and accordingly he may seek to change some discordant elements more to his desires. But what he cannot change, he accepts without emotional disturbance.

Honesty With Yourself

To be honest with yourself means that you accept yourself with your faults as well as your strengths. In fact, it would be difficult to improve your personality unless you first recognized your inadequacies. Self-acceptance, for better or for worse, involves an acknowledgment of your more impulsive drives. For example, it would be unrealistic to deny that you have sexual desires. Courage and honesty require that your passions and hatreds be brought fully to your consciousness. In this context, you can handle them for your own welfare and that of others.

Adjusting to the World

Facing reality does not only involve honest self-knowledge; one must also in many instances adjust to the world as it is. A fool is one who assumes that he can always change the world and then sulks because that world refuses to change. Equally unwise is the

28

person who refuses to see that injustice, cruelty, and exploitation of the weak have always existed and possibly will continue. This does not mean that we must not seek to redress the wrongs of our society, but it does imply that we must accept what we cannot change. If a person must remain unhappy until all wrongs are corrected, then he must inevitably remain unhappy for the rest of his life.

It is disastrous to our well-being to assume that everybody is trustworthy. You can lose all your money if you have complete trust in your fellowmen. Face the fact that no matter how idealistic you may be, there are still dishonest people. Adjusting to reality means that you are not gullible enough to believe that all people are honorable. You accept what you cannot change in this regard as in many other aspects of your world that are far from good. In your personal life and that of the community, you may have to pay a heavy price for looking at the world through rose-colored glasses.

On the other hand, you have the bitter and unfortunate pessimist who sees nothing but evil. Certainly it is unrealistic to view things as worse than they actually are. There is a kind of personality characterized by unwarranted suspicion, jealousy, envy, and a tendency to blame others and ascribe evil motives to everyone. These traits interfere with a person's ability to maintain satisfactory interpersonal relations. Indeed there are people with evil designs; but the paranoiac places everybody in the same category. There is a wide difference between complete trust and complete mistrust, but in either case the person does not confront reality but distorts it. The chronic pessimist's world isolates him from fellowmen who do not share his twisted views.

Similarly maladjusted is the chronic optimist who is so elated in his own world that he is ever carried away, prattling of his grandiose plans that can never come true.

Contrary to the unrealistic optimist and the opposite unjustified pessimist, the normal person sees his surroundings in varying degrees of evil and good. He must accept some aspects of life because he cannot change them. The past, for example, cannot be altered, the death of a parent or lover cannot be undone. People disagree, per-

fection is never reached, and finally laws of nature are there to
stay. It is as absurd for one to try to fly without a plane as it is
for a mentally retarded person to practice law or to be licensed
as a physician.

Some people, of course, do minimize being hurt by refusing to face
reality, living in their own concept of reality. The manic person
who writes checks without funds to back them certainly enjoys his
"philanthropy." For the normal person, however, there is a price
to pay in that there must be money in the bank before he can sign
his name to checks. Generally, therefore, facing reality is not easy.
But there are advantages in keeping one's feet on the ground, in
evaluating your world as it is instead of having it as you fancy it
ought to be.

Avoiding Disappointments

If you are a sentimental optimist, you are apt to become disillusioned, then cynical. A person who is too naive frequently is
misled by unsophisticated idealism, taking a too rosy view of people
and the universe. Some people want to remake society overnight,
eliminate wars at one stroke out of pure love for the human race,
rehabilitate all criminals because basically they are all lovable
creatures. Unfortunately the world is rarely changed by mere
sentimentality. The extreme idealist often becomes demoralized and
embittered. Such a tragic outcome can be avoided by tempering
your dreams with cold facts.

If you expect too much of life, you will be disappointed. On the
other hand, if you expect too little you will invite boredom. The
person who avoids these two extremes is prepared to accept
reality, expecting neither more nor less than life has to offer. He
doesn't seek things beyond his reach, nor does he expect too little
of life.

Too many people have suffered because they have assumed that
honest effort is enough, that one is promoted purely on merit, that
as skills and experience improve there will automatically be more

money, more responsible positions. What happens to those people when life does not turn out as they expected? They become bitter and overwhelmed with disillusionment.

The secret is to be neither an incurable optimist nor a chronic pessimist. The world is not perfect, people have weaknesses. You must, if you are to avoid disappointment, view the world as neither good nor evil—while contrarily it can be both at the same time. Man is neither an angel nor a devil; and yet at different times and circumstances he can play the part of either one.

The Reality Principle

There is nothing wrong about seeking pleasure. In fact, the more alive you are the more you will be able to enjoy yourself. However, it is not wise to grasp pleasure on the spur of the moment without realizing that the greatest pleasure may ultimately be yours only after postponing the joys of the moment. The reality principle and the pleasure principle have been recognized as follows: Often one has to postpone pleasures now in order to gain a greater pleasure later. The process is to judge whether or not it is wise to enjoy oneself to the limit in the present or to sacrifice something in order to reap greater reward in the future. The mark of those who cannot evaluate reality is this very act of taking now instead of waiting for more satisfaction later. The immature and undisciplined child does not visualize tomorrow; he wants what he wants now.

Some people are similarly immature in that, for example, they cannot understand that to reap the rewards of a skill or profession they must first devote a time of study to it. Such an attitude denies the fact that one must often take pain before realizing lasting pleasure. In realistic thinking there is first the wish, the goal, and then the planning toward that goal. On the other hand, those who would take their pleasure now are dominated by a sort of childish thinking that seeks to make dreams come true without sacrifice or effort.

Certainly spontaneous pleasure is accepted by normal people;

life is too short and in some sense too unpredictable not to enjoy it. However, there is a difference between the fun-loving person who can also plan for more meaningful pleasures in years to come, and one who can say, "Eat, drink, and be merry and tomorrow be damned."

Unpleasant Facts

Obviously one can appreciate pleasant facts. The bright side of life should certainly be noted when there is so much good to be enjoyed. But there is also the need to educate yourself to acknowledge the unpleasant part of your existence. It is too easy for one to evade harsh reality, and this is particularly true of mentally disturbed persons who refuse to see the facts of life.

Clear-eyed and unprejudiced recognition of stern and ugly facets of the world helps us to cope with them. However, those who complain about all things being wrong are not realists insofar as they see only the gloomy part of reality. The true realist takes a different view. He includes both the unhappy and the happy parts of his experiences.

There is a group of artists and commentators who call themselves realists—in the sense that they present the real facts of life. However, they insist on describing only one side of our society, the side that is demeaning and dirty, low and degrading. They speak as if our country were a combination of slums and poverty with nothing in between. These modern preachers of doom and decay reject all fixed values: There is no God, no immortality or purpose, no real hope. Novelists wallow in marital conflicts, in criminality as the sum total of life. It is the style to debunk heroes, people in high places. Even when somewhat justified, they go beyond such justification until only the greed and evil of men remain. All this is done in the name of truth, but it provides only a distorted and partial view of reality.

It is difficult to be impartial in this deluge of cynicism. And yet mental health is largely determined by the ability to steer a middle course by which we can face the reality of a mixture of evil and of the many factors that exist to our advantage in a free and dynamic society. Perhaps a rose is more beautiful when contrasted with something ugly, but it would be tragic if we were so fascinated with the obscene that we failed to see the beauty more prominent in the foreground.

Some people seem to have been born reformers. All their lives, they find the world out of joint. They are too busy seeking the evil in others to see any in themselves. These are the folks who would hang every criminal because they are essentially afraid of their own conscience, fearful that it might be exposed unless they fight ruthlessly against any perpetrator of antisocial acts.

It is ironic that much of our progress toward more civilized conduct has been instigated by people with over-strict consciences. However, with increasing self-understanding and self-confidence you will be able to decide whether the climate of opinion is due to hysteria or to a well thought out course of action tending to augment human happiness.

CHAPTER IV

Training for a Good Life

Young people are generally eager for self-improvement, and they do not hesitate to accept guidance on their own terms. In other words, they do not relish being told, but they are ready to consider whatever advice may be offered by someone who respects their autonomy and their right to make up their own minds.

The Need for Security

During the first two years of life the infant should be indulged. This practice is based on the child's need to build a sense of security and a feeling that the world is benign and protective. Once the sense of security and faith and confidence in his parents has been established, the child is ready to embark on experiences that provide minor frustrations and later even major deprivations for short periods of time to implant the ability to withstand obstacles to his desires. This is termed "frustration tolerance" by psychologists.

With the encouragement of his parents, the child is introduced gently to more hardships that are necessary for a human being to get along in this world. In this manner, without fear, he is encouraged to withstand and overcome difficulties.

It is essential that a person learn that he can trust his environment and that he can to a great extent courageously control it. Parents can help to develop this sort of confidence by not deceiving the child with false promises. They must create conditions that will enable their offspring to develop self-confidence. Inconsistency is the enemy of this process.

Unwise parents must be on guard against laughing at the child for being too trusting. Later, with greater confidence, the child must learn that faith in others is not always desirable. Ridicule is the worst way to teach early habits that ultimately may prove disadvantageous.

If your upbringing has been lacking in wisdom and tact, you can examine your present fears and lack of confidence. You can trace their sources and thus become better able to handle them, using whatever guidance and information you may be able to obtain as a young adult.

Self-discipline

In order to develop in the child the habit of postponing pleasure on occasion, it is necessary to provide practice, to create an environment in which he can experiment. This is a lesson that the emotionally unstable adult has failed to grasp. If he does not receive what he wants at a given time, the reaction is one of disappointment and hostility. As we have seen, the capacity to postpone instant pleasure in order to receive it at a more appropriate time is a mark of mature behavior.

To be well adjusted a person must have the ability to seek long-range objectives. Self-discipline also implies the will to meet obligations even under difficult circumstances. This at times necessitates the putting aside of personal wishes to meet social demands.

Doubtless the most valuable part of education is to learn the habit of doing things you have to do whether you like to do them or not. Many people fail to acquire this habit, to their disadvantage and the weakening of their personality.

Some psychologists have pointed out that modern education does not emphasize a sense of duty. Many schools encourage youngsters to do what they want to do. This approach is a reversal of the regimentation of an older type of education that was apt to foster inhibited and frustrated personalities. The newer school, on the other hand, may be producing students who are concerned solely with their self-interest without considering the rights of others. A different type of education will perhaps be evolved by the younger generation, eliminating the inadequacies of the two extremes.

Meanwhile you can learn to discipline yourself to enjoy what you do have. You will then not waste your time hoping for the unattainable.

How High to Aspire?

In our competitive society, many people seek achievement that is beyond their reach. And yet happiness depends largely upon realistic levels of aspiration.

A child's standards generally reflect those of his parents—or what his parents expect of him. In order to offset their own limited socio-economic level, they frequently impose standards that cannot be met by their offspring, both in school work and in later adaptation as an adult. In the process the child may have been prepared for a hopeless perfectionism and subsequent disappointment. Many people have been guided by unwise parents into careers without regard to their wishes and talents.

The parent who has the happiness of his child at heart should realize his own fallibility as an adviser and encourage the youngster to make his own decision on the basis of information obtained from a professional psychologist or counselor. The vocational counselor—usually reached at school or university clinics—can evaluate a person's aptitudes and interests. The client is then advised of his abilities and suitabilities for a given career. Such consultation and testing can prevent a person from selecting a field of work for which he is unsuited.

Satisfaction in lifework comes from a realistic evaluation of personal assets. However, if a person has aspirations beyond his abilities, disappointment is apt to occur. A high school student who has barely made his way through, with particular weakness in mathematics, would certainly find it difficult to become an accountant. On the other hand, similar disaster may await the more talented youngster who is unwilling to use his potentialities and to put forth the effort necessary to develop them.

Happiness is more easily attained if you concentrate on improvement rather than on perfection. It is best to seek gradual improvement instead of seeking to take one giant step. Keep your eye on today's progress in comparison with yesterday's instead of measuring how far you still have to go. Intermediate goals are best because they give you a sense of progress. The successful person sets each objective a little beyond his last achievement.

Too high a goal, although flattering to the ego, offers greater risks. Repeated failures tend to lower motivation. On the other hand too low a goal, although it may easily be reached, will not satisfy because of insufficient challenge.

People differ in their reactions to success and failure. The neurotic may be afraid of both success and failure. He fears success because others might envy his achievement and subsequently deprive him of affection that he wants. Accordingly, the neurotic may choose a lower goal to fit in with the vast majority, thus avoiding offending anybody.

It is very important for you to experience success. Being successful will increase your self-confidence, alertness, and cheerfulness. Failure, on the other hand, is apt to make you insecure, dull, and morose.

Too high standards in school or at work without regard to individual differences are detrimental because they tend to induce failure in many people. It is wise to establish levels appropriate to each person, thus assuring success in a greater number of cases.

You must learn that your ambitions should match as closely as possible your abilities, talents, and potentialities. It is rare today for one to rise from a lowly position to a highly paid executive position, and yet more youngsters are preparing for so-called white-collar jobs than there are vacancies available. Almost three-quarters of job holders today are engaged in manual and technical employment.

It may be discouraging to a college graduate with a degree in Arts to find out that he is likely to receive a lower wage than that being paid to a laborer in the Sanitation Department in any of our large cities. A college professor may well receive a lower salary after years of experience than that paid to a plumber with union membership. These facts are presented not to discourage aspiration to the more professional fields, but rather to point out that it is far from being a disgrace to prepare for a skilled job rather than one that seems to carry more prestige. A satisfying life is a better aim than a particular career based on keeping up with the Joneses.

Practical Standards

Setting impossible goals is a frequent cause of disappointment. To assume that anything can be perfect is unrealistic. There is no such thing as absolute honesty or absolute loyalty. Aspiration based on ideals that are unattainable can lead to maladjustment and other difficulties such as overconscientiousness and faultfinding. Some people suffer from too severe a conscience fostered by unwise parents, clergymen, and educators. We should temper our moral aspirations, the strictness of our conscience, within limits set by ourselves and not by those whose moral values may be outmoded.

Distinguishing the Real from the Unreal

If you become addicted to unreality, after a while you may ultimately lose touch with reality itself, daydreaming instead of striving toward reasonable goals. Some popular writers who claim to have psychological insight say that if we only could change our thoughts, everything would turn out all right. All you have to do is to think positively and the world will be yours. But on the contrary mere wishing will not get what you want. Suppose, for example, you come to a river; there you sit on the bank wishing to get across. Wish and think positively as long as you like, still the river continues to flow and you're stuck on this side. Now let us assume that you finally realize you need more than mere thinking along unrealistic lines, and you decide to tackle the problem on realistic principles.

Instead of sitting with your impractical and unrealistic approach, you begin to evaluate the situation. If there were a bridge you could get across; however, there is no bridge. Finally, after having taken many factors into consideration, you make the crossing by pushing ahead of you a fallen log that you found floating on the edge of the stream—and you succeed.

Wishing does motivate your actions, but mere wishing is unrealistic. The facts of life are still unchanged until you decide to think realistically; in other words, doing something about your problem.

A person may envision wealth in contrast to his poverty; he may dream of getting out of crowded quarters and wish for decent living space. But all his wishing for improvement is in vain unless he decides to do something practical and realistic, such as getting training for a good job.

The drudgery of our daily life may be lessened by romanticizing boring data and glamorizing ordinary routines. In fact fantasies may make our daily existence less grinding and even beautiful. An unrealistic point of view in moderation can enrich our lives,—and certainly advocating realism is not to imply that dreams and beautiful thoughts should be eliminated. Great artists live largely in their fantasies alone. The greatest artists indeed are those who turn their dreams into monuments, pictures, novels, and art that can be shared by others. A person who clings to his dreams without actualizing them for his fellowmen to grasp and to enjoy can never be a real artist because he does not share with others; he remains hidden only to die finally with his dreams never having materialized into the world of reality.

For a young man to admire a beautiful girl, an actress of television and screen, is a pleasant diversion if the dream girl does not detract from the girl next door whom he will possibly marry. If through his fantasy he expects his Debra to look like the actress of his dreams, he is in for a rude awakening when the wife appears in curlers after a day of housecleaning. If his thinking is realistic, he will be content with an average spouse and stop visualizing her as another Farah Fawcett. He should be allowed to dream if he comes down to earth in his daily contacts.

The girl who sighs and pines for the virile, handsome hero as depicted in a romantic story is apt to be severely shocked to discover that the ordinary guy is quite different. Her fantasies of manhood must be replaced by the reality of the man who frequently comes home too tired to make love to her.

Glamorizing excessively is apt to lead to disillusionment. Similarly, going into a career that seems to yield public acclaim may be equally costly. For example, one may admire a television detective. It all seems so thrilling and adventurous. But those in the field agree that it can be routine, boring, and frustrating. In some professions the glamor is not so real behind the scenes. If the sweat, the uncertainty, the worry behind an actor's work were widely known, the glamor might be less.

Some people are fascinated by far places such as South Sea isles. Reality, however, discloses the discomforts, the inconvenience, and the suffering of natives all combining to deglamorize the dreamy Pacific and the tropics of our own hemisphere. The beaches turn out to be coarse sand, and the pretty girls in the travelogues frequently have neither swirling grass skirts nor teeth.

To accept myths and unreality is dangerous, since a time may come when reality shocks us into rude awakening.

Young people with sincere ideals who actually seek to match them against the world frequently are disillusioned, and their optimism is replaced by cynicism. It is often a sad story, and yet it teaches them a basic lesson—that they must distinguish between reality and unreality. Their dreams are wonderful but ultimately deceiving unless they are willing to work to make them come true.

How Much Can You Tolerate?

Life is not necessarily designed for human comfort. We must learn to withstand frustrations and avoid certain people. However, the person who is emotionally healthy learns to put up with the inevitable. He will deal with what can be altered and accept what he cannot change, resigning himself to the latter and irremediable aspects of his existence.

There is much that is disagreeable in our world. There are quarrels, misunderstandings, loneliness, terrible weather, failures, accidents, sickness, the long-distance call that does not come, bills, letters that go astray, broken promises, and a host of other causes of distress and tension.

It takes very little to upset some people. A leaky faucet can make home intolerably uncomfortable for an oversensitive person. A woman may be almost hysterical at discovering a run in her pantyhose. Such people have a low level of frustration tolerance; they are too easily upset when things do not turn out as expected.

Fortunately anyone can raise his ability to withstand frustration by developing a "thicker skin." The secret of tolerance is to get accustomed to irritations as a habit, to desensitize one's reaction to the disappointments that are inevitable in the routine of living. For example, a child can get rid of his fear of darkness by playing a fascinating game with a person he can trust. He enjoys himself so much that he forgets to be afraid. An actor can get rid of stage fright by succeeding in lesser parts, thus gradually overcoming his fears through greater successes.

Unfortunately, some well-meaning parents actually train their children to become failures. Although this is not done consciously, it engenders in the child a sense of defeat and inadequacy. All of us have met the so-called brat who assumes that the world owes him a living. He is cocky and demanding to hide his feeling of inferiority. Any job that he undertakes ends in disaster because he has not developed the ability to get along with people, especially with authority figures, against who he nurses an anger beyond his control.

Essentially, this person has not been trained to withstand frustrations and hardships. His parents, perhaps in an effort to hide lack of real love for the child, have given him everything he wanted. He was protected from the suffering and the cruelty of the world—with tragic consequences in succeeding years.

Strange as it may seem, some frustrations and hard times are necessary to develop our ability to cope with our environment and gain a sense of achievement.

CHAPTER V

Running Away

There are ways to deal with difficulties or unpleasant situations. You can face the annoying reality bravely, you can change it for the better, or you can seek to escape from it.

It has been pointed out that a person can build up his ability to withstand frustration, and that one should accept what cannot be changed. The hope that some disagreeable situation will be altered and that you yourself may be an instrument in improving society is not ignored. But the point to emphasize is that you should not become thoroughly disappointed and bitter because you cannot get what is unattainable. Sometimes we must accommodate ourselves to what we dislike.

A person who will accept neither the inevitable nor the possibility of change may seek to escape from the whole process, to toss aside reality and find refuge in a variety of ways, to run away from annoying circumstances.

Building Dream Castles

Daydreaming provides flight from reality through one's imagination. We project our limited experiences onto conquering heroes. If such a practice were followed by efforts to be bolder and to take productive action, the urge to imitate heroes might be a healthful form of play. But if dreams are a substitute for achievement, the process is one of escape. Excessive daydreaming encourages running away from reality, turning away from real life. The psychotic is so absorbed with his world of fantasy that he lives completely in that world, no longer able to distinguish the realities about him. In fact his dreams, whether good or bad, become the only things real to him, and the outside environment and people hardly exist.

Nothing can be more useless than to dream about what might

have been: If only you had married the right guy, if you had not spent your money foolishly, if you had learned to play tennis, if you had selected another field of work, if only you had been wiser—and on and on, dreaming of past mistakes, regretting. Lamenting what could have happened is a waste of time and has no place in an emotionally healthy person.

More subtle kinds of daydreaming occur to avid television and movie fans and to those addicted to romantic novels. This sort of vicarious experience can be diverting as a substitute for dull routine. Soap operas on television relieve boredom because they are so vivid. There is no exertion in this recreation, and no time to judge the practicality of portrayed events or situations. Television intrigues while washing dishes, but it does not develop critical thinking; it dulls the intellect and perhaps encourages a sad contact between the make-believe and the ordinary routine of vacuuming the living room.

Maybe the daydreamer would get more fun out of life if he or she paid more attention to other people, enjoying human relationships instead of seeking solace in fantasies.

To the neurotic, the present is secondary. He lives in the past or the future. Surely next year will be better. I shall meet the ideal mate. There are so many things to put off until tomorrow. I'll cut down on my smoking, maybe give up pot—as soon as I feel less tense. Maybe next week I'll start exercising, slim down, take a vacation, or even go to church.

Escape into the future is a malady of the emotionally disturbed person who does not have the courage to do what he should do today. It is a mirage that remains as long as we postpone responsibilities. How much better it is to tackle what is desirable, to work for the accomplishing of goals instead of deluding oneself that tomorrow will bring all to fruition. Tomorrow never really comes, because when it is here it becomes the present. The now is the vital part of our lives, not yesterday or the day after today.

Escape into the Intellect

Some timid professors spend their lives amid dusty tomes, annoyed at any disturbance from outside their studies. They complain about the pressure of "Publish or perish." In other words, they resent sharing what knowledge they may possess, particularly the necessity at times to teach undergraduate courses. College and university study can become a sort of neurosis, a refuge from the everyday environment of the average person. Outside the ivory tower of universities, there are others who through presumably wide reading and study avoid the cutthroat competition in the market-place.

Some people would rather read about life than live it. There is nothing wrong with reading, keeping up with current events, trends, and thought. Great literature and even popular books can keep us in contact with prevailing movements in our society. Excessive immersion in books and scholarship, however, can be an escape from reality, an avoidance of circumstances tending to isolation. Over-indulgence in things academic can be due to a panicky fear of people. The literary occupation may be an attempt to hide in the realm of ideas. Those who try to escape may continue indefinitely in college attendance, ultimately becoming professors and teachers and thereby continuing to impress their hearers with profound erudition. Some of these scholars have never dirtied their hands with competition in the real world.

Having taught at four universities, the author has seen the impractical bickerings of his colleagues, wondering if the pettiness often displayed could survive in industry. Not all professional scholars belong in this category; but perhaps only a small minority in our universities do worthwhile research. Most others share irrelevancies with colleagues through so-called reports of research that are rarely read, in spite of the fact that such publications weigh heavily in gaining academic promotion.

Reading and other sources of intellectual stimulation are necessary for self-improvement; but when they become an excessive form of withdrawing from people they turn into a pernicious alienation from social relationships. The emotionally healthy person will enjoy reading good books, be inspired by art in its various forms, and be inspired by his imagination. But these moments of solitude and reaching deep within oneself will be supplementary to the deeper satisfaction of **friendship**, of sharing richly with others the sense of belonging that only human contact can bring.

The Snob

Loneliness is one of the most widespread conditions in our society. In some cases loneliness is engendered by circumstances beyond the control of the person, but more frequently the person brings it upon himself. Closely related to the intellectualism described above is the device of purposely isolating oneself from other people. We have read of hermits living alone by choice, shunning people. Living in their fort of loneliness, they evade all the baffling problems of human intercourse.

Less isolated than the hermit is the perpetual knocker. He pans all organizations and declares that the world is going to hell on a dozen wheels with madmen as the drivers. With snobbish sneers, he looks with condescension on those who are still close to reality. By considering himself superior to those who manage to put up with the nonsense of the world, he looks down from his mount of discontent, pitying the poor slobs who manage to like their work and love their friends. By turning up his nose, the alienated person saves himself the trouble of close emotional relationships, friends, and responsibilities.

The Phony

Some people circumvent reality by taking nothing seriously. They are as counterfeit as a wooden nickel. They think of themselves as too sophisticated to feel sad when the occasion demands it, ever retaining a lighthearted demeanor, irresponsibly gay to avoid being emotionally involved or having to meet their obligations. Others are viewed as suckers when concerned about duty and associates. Everything is a laughing matter. They cannot allow themselves to be disappointed. Sorrow is for the weak and stupid. As far as they are concerned, life is a ball, an endless comedy.

Indeed, it is at times necessary to cover up our deep and varying moods in order not to impose upon those who might be disturbed by them. But generally it is best to be ourselves, and not imitate the psychopathic person whose feelings are either absent or hidden in a pseudo and unreal never-may-care attitude.

The Runaway

Many people literally run away from their responsibilities. Eighth Avenue in New York City finds countless young people who have left their homes in various parts of the country, ending as drifters and easy marks for pimps and others who prey on the restless and the lost. Thousands of others flee from their troubles. Children leave home because they can no longer stand their parents. A man takes to the road trying to avoid the burdens of family and the heavy demands of society. The migratory worker frequently has chosen his way of life voluntarily, working when he feels like it, then pushing onward to another location. A tramp simply does not want to work unless he has to do so. He just wants to travel, not knowing what he is looking for but definitely knowing that he does not want to work. A bum wants neither travel nor work; he merely wants to stay put and vegetate, preferably with a bottle of cheap wine.

There are others on a higher socioeconomic level, moneyed people who are ever planning their next trip to Florida, the Riviera, or the far corners of the earth, ever seeking escape from reality, to duck their responsibilities at home.

Getting Married

Marriage is still one of our most alluring institutions, but when it is used as a means of escape from burdensome circumstances, it generally leads to unhappiness and divorce. Some girls marry to get away from their families or to escape from a tedious job. For a desperate female any man will do as long as he supports her and provides a home, a car, and money for clothes. However, the girl who marries merely to get away from a bad situation often develops hatred for her rescuer, knowing that she is trapped in a blind alley.

Finally fed up with her boring husband, she seeks an out through the divorce court.

A man can be similarly trapped. Tired of eating in hotels and restaurants, wanting a housekeeper and a cook, not to mention a good bedfellow, he takes the plunge not considering personality or motives—merely to escape. On the other hand, the man may decide to remain a bachelor for a corresponding need to evade responsibilities. A woman may also stay away from marriage for the same reasons.

It seems obvious that there are many ways of escaping human relationships. If more couples tried to analyze their real motives before marriage, the divorce courts would be less crowded. Even in our modern time with greater tolerance in family and sexual mores, old-fashioned love, trust, and compatibility are still the only bases for a happy marriage.

Religion as Escape

Even if it be false that, as Karl Marx said, religion is the opiate of the masses, it still is true that religion can be used as an escape from reality. Not that it is meant to be so, but rather that a person may blame God for his shortcomings and laziness instead of doing something constructive about his situation.

There is nevertheless a great deal in the churches' teaching that man is essentially good, that there is love from God, that one should forgive sin, that immortal life awaits us.

The escapist unfortunately assumes that God will take care of him, that he need not plan and exert himself. He can withdraw from this world because the next one will automatically reward him for doing little while on earth. The really religious person is a worker who says that God will take care of those who help themselves and their neighbors.

It is far from sacrilegious to point out that God could not grant all requests. It would be difficult to answer a prayer for rain by farmers and another prayer for sunshine for a county fair in the same area. Many lazy people would gladly have God do their work

48 COPING WITH YOUR EMOTIONS

for them instead of seeking to improve their own lot. Obviously, if there be a God, he would certainly not approve of this sort of dependency. Using religion as a means of escape from reality must in the end defeat the essence of religion, which stresses responsibility for one's actions.

Another aspect of religious behavior that is a definite means of avoiding temptation and the will to resist evil is the ascetic's way of life. Some sincerely religious persons choose convents and monasteries to worship God. These are deeply religious people who give up the pleasures of the world for a higher purpose. However, the church does not look with favor on those who enter a life of self-denial and celibacy as a means of escape, because they embrace the monastic life solely motivated by fear of the rigors of ordinary society.

Increasingly churches of various denominations are teaching a gospel of reform, leading a frontal attack on social injustices. The words of Christ and prophets are now heard in the marketplace with ever-mounting stress on the realities of society.

In spite of the more pragmatic approach to religion today, we must not forget that man needs a faith to help him escape from the sorrows that he might have to bear. The grieving parent of a dead child can find solace in the belief that some day he will be reunited with him in the hereafter. Fortunately no one has even been able to prove the nonexistence of immortality.

Drugs and Booze

Drugs and alcohol can be placed in the same category of intoxicants. Why is liquor regarded as acceptable and in fact part of the social scene when marijuana—which is possibly no more addictive or toxic—is condemned by law? We have the same situation that faced our fathers under Prohibition, which led to organized crime in the 1920's and early 1930's. This is not a plea for legislation against nonaddictive drugs, but rather to point out the idiocy of our system of laws, which often perpetuates unreality in the name of unjustified morality.

Nevertheless drugs and alcohol are consumed to get a "high" and to loosen inhibitions. Nothing pleases a psychologist more than to hear one of his patients say, "I don't need pot or grass to get high anymore. I'm not afraid to be myself, and I have a better time, while my friends look ridiculous, making me feel sorry for them because they cannot have fun without drinks or joints."

Millions of people drink or smoke—often both—to drown or forget their sorrows or to ease themselves over difficult situations. Drunkenness offers a quick and convenient means of escape, particularly for people who are very vulnerable to stress.

Inebriation enables people to accept the routine difficulties of their lives. They react inadequately to deprivations and frequently are overwhelmed by their defeats. Shy and ill at ease in social life, insecure, through drink or drugs they shut out reality and achieve a temporary loosening of inhibitions. Sexually they are frequently promiscuous, followed by a letdown and even periods of impotency. The belief that a hard-drinking man is virile and daring is only half true. He might flaunt his masculinity in a burst of bravado, seeming full of life and aggression, only to wither away too soon. Drug addicts as well as alcoholics do not live up to expectation and are in the long run little interested in sex. They tend to be very free in talk and short on action.

The person who can relax only by getting high—either with drugs or with too many drinks—ultimately finds that his life is similar to a roller coaster. He is the "life of the party"; his conversation and ideas flow (to himself) full of wisdom and depth. But there is always the morning after, the hangover, the guilt about his slurring remarks, the lack of inhibition followed by the knowledge that he made a fool of himself. We are speaking not about the occasional drink or the sharing of a joint, but rather about the alcoholic or the drug addict who has largely lost control of himself. He has all the symptoms of the manic-depressive, swinging from high to low until his true self has been effaced, leaving him suspended in a world of unreality between hell and heaven.

The tragedy of addiction is that the time of well-being lasts only a little while, with sober reality in the wings to return with more difficulties, guilt, and physical pain.

People indulge to be more sociable, to speak more freely, to hide their embarrassment, and to forget their troubles. Because spontaneity is so difficult for a neurotic person, the temptation to moderate use of drugs or alcohol is great indeed. The more insecure he is, the stronger becomes the allure. But while many manage to remain moderate in this indulgence, too many go on to become addicts. It has been claimed that use of marijuana leads to heavier drugs such as heroin. If this is true, however, it must be that the addict was mentally ill in the first place and that he would have found some other means of self-destruction if hard drugs had not been available.

The heavy drinker turns to alcohol to banish anxiety. Many people are mentally disturbed, and it is this accompanying anxiety that is the root of the problem. Such people have a low frustration tolerance level; they cannot "take it" as more emotionally healthy persons can.

Intoxication is a way out for chronic alcoholics and drug addicts. They cannot face reality. Too sensitive to their anxieties and unable to bear them, they seek temporary relief that becomes ever more difficult to achieve. The secret of avoiding this tragedy, of course, is to trace the source of anxiety in order to eliminate it through self-improvement, or to seek the professional help of a psychologist or psychiatrist.

Emotional Disorders

No one is always satisfied with his world, and nobody likes anxieties and the frustrations that cause them. The facts of life do not lend themselves to our wishes in general. The manner in which these conditions are handled distinguishes between the normal person and the mentally ill.

The neurotic person is less able to cope than is the emotionally well adjusted. He must have much support in his many disappointments. His very ailment is a means of avoiding reality. Daydreaming is paramount in his life-style; he gets much satisfaction out of it, hoping, always hoping that his longings and wishes will obliterate reality. The neurotic is well aware that he is different from the average person, although he admits this with a great deal of reluctance.

The neurotic person often seeks to hide his conflicts by being unobtrusive, perhaps choosing work that allows him to be apart from others. He may engage in a hobby in which seclusion is permissible, or he may become a drunkard or a drug addict. He may develop habits that serve as defenses, making him look peculiar to other people—always wearing a hat, for example, because he cannot face the idea of being partially bald.

Nevertheless the neurotic person—other than the one who gives himself up entirely to drugs or alcohol—more often continues at an occupation that is frequently below his capability and intellectual level. If he is a bookkeeper, he continues at his task, but meanwhile he dreams of glory someday. In his imagination he pictures himself as a great artist, although he never tries to write a novel, sculpt a statue, or paint a picture. He knows the difference between right and wrong, and in fact he may be overconcerned about his moral conduct and the need to stay within the law.

Whereas the neurotic is fully aware of the world and wishes to get away from it, the psychotic is so repelled by reality that he takes steps to deny it. He has lost the ability to tolerate frustration, and his escape has been total or almost total. The psychologist can point out to the neurotic that his world is unreal, and he will agree because he knows that his behavior is inappropriate. On the other hand, there is no use or purpose in pointing out to the psychotic that what he imagines is unreal, because his world is completely his own and he sees nothing wrong with his attitudes and thoughts. His conflicts were so painful that with the beginning of his psychosis he put aside and eliminated reality entirely. Ultimately he is not aware that his world is different from reality, and in fact it becomes more real for him than the outside world, and he conducts himself accordingly. If he imagines himself as the President, he acts as if he were in that position. If he believes himself very rich, he throws money out the window or into the street. He can always get more from the gold mines that he believes exist in his own private domain. All he has to do is to wire the Treasurer of the United States, who will advance all the credit he wants, using his imaginary gold holdings as collateral.

The world of the psychotic's own making, born of his sick imagination, is not always so harmless. He may hear voices that command him to do evil deeds; he may feel that a water pipe has been tapped with some electronic device to spy upon him. Frequently he is not violent, but his conduct is irrational and impossible to understand. As a consequence, he must be segregated because he is incapable of knowing the difference between real and unreal, between right and wrong. For that reason, if he commits a crime, the law assumes that he was not responsible for his antisocial behavior and he is generally sent to a mental institution instead of jail.

Neurosis and psychosis are obviously means of escaping from reality. The most complete of all escapes is suicide, but a psychosis allows a person to exist in a never-ending dream. The unfortunate victim prefers his delusions to the frustrations of the real world. He cancels his personal identity and breaks with the harshness of his conflicts, with society, family, and the risks of love.

One of the most effective means of escaping from an unsatisfactory existence is to become involved in helping others. A person with a cause is concerned about correcting great wrongs: the improvement of living conditions for all Americans, the elimination of corruption, crooked politics, and ignorance.

A capitalist society, it is argued, seeks escape from a lesser state or condition to a higher one by competing with others. The sense of achievement is immediately felt, or its opposite is discerned as failure. The tendency, then, is for a competitive society to impose responsibility on the individual.

In a communistic society, escape from an unsatisfactory existence is presumed to take place by serving the state, thus distancing the individual from a sense of immediate achievement.

To escape from poverty, ignorance, injustice, and unbearable conflicts is commendable. To escape from self-responsibility, on the other hand, is destructive and self-defeating.

CHAPTER VI

Improving Our World

The aim of this chapter is to show how conditions can be improved to lessen frustrations, thus reducing the urge to escape from reality. Some psychologists seem to imply that a well-adjusted person is one who is satisfied with things as they are. In stating that we must accept some aspects of our existence that cannot be changed, the implication was not that we should not seek to change things that are within our power to improve. The phrase "a well-adjusted personality" implies on the contrary one who knows that he cannot alter the law of gravity, nor can he eliminate the evil in the hearts of men. However, as a well-adjusted person, he will realize that one of the main avenues to comparative happiness is to achieve, to love, and to mold social and economic conditions nearer to his heart's desire and that of his fellow-humans.

Facing reality, therefore, does not mean that we must accept all things as they are. The emotionally healthy person is realistic enough to see the inadequacies, the injustices, the criminality that can be changed in order to make reality easier to bear.

The realist does not seek to escape reality—things as they really are. He observes what is wrong and seeks to change circumstances to improve both himself and society. Our job as dynamic individuals is to get along as best we can with things that actually exist while at the same time trying to create a better environment in which to live. The emotionally alive person sees things as the actual conditions exist, but he also seeks to ameliorate his own lot and that of others.

Some Progress

It is easy to enunciate the shortcomings of our society: the insecurity created by an arms race, the threat of nuclear war, poverty

53

among a large portion of our society, our cities plagued by crime and cynicism, unemployment and inflation, the possibility of a depression —and many other problems that mar our world.

However, we must not stop there and sit back in unalterable pessimism. Never in the history of mankind has there been greater progress, brought about mostly by people who strive for positive action rather than negative reaction.

Medical science and other helping professions have done much to reduce diseases, to prolong life. Whether or not a longer life means a better life has yet to be decided. But certainly the person who is less affected by pain and who has peace of mind will appreciate more years than he would have had when tuberculosis was incurable. Infant mortality has been greatly reduced, saving much sorrow for those who love their children. Crippling diseases such as poliomyelitis and smallpox have been practically eliminated among those who take advantage of medical prevention.

In spite of unemployment and poverty in sections of our population, it is still true that the living standard in this country is comparatively high. The bulk of Americans are well fed and enjoy a higher educational standard than the people of many other nations.

Progress has been made in working conditions, with greater awareness of the need to increase satisfaction on the job. Unions have led in demanding more security for employees. Management is beginning to understand that human factors in industry are vital in augmenting productivity. Boredom and monotony on the job have in some industries been lowered by shifting workers from routine tasks to more varied assignments, alternating with different projects. Personnel policies have changed to reward conscientious workers with monetary and fringe benefits. Vocational guidance in educational institutions and public and governmental employment agencies is helping people to obtain work suitable to their skills and interests. The work that one does can do much to engender a sense of satisfaction.

In spite of the mounting divorce rate, people continue to get married. The fact is that an easy separation may contribute to a couple's happiness by emancipating incompatible mates and giving them a second opportunity to a fuller life. Marriage counselors or psychotherapists are now licensed in many states to help couples achieve happier adjustment to husbands and wives. There are many sex counselors ready to offer their professional knowledge toward a better understanding of sexual difficulties. A healthier concept of sex saves many marriages and improves love relationships.

Family life, while weakening in some respects, is no longer ruled by the autocratic husband and father. Wives and children assert their rights, and the family forming a democratic unit doubtless provides for greater self-responsibility. Some civic leaders claim that lack of obedience in the home has resulted in a general let-down of morals and a tendency toward laxness in community affairs. Others point out that never in our history have so many people taken part in determining their own political future. If the family as a social institution is being attacked for its weaknesses, it may be because we are in the process of a peaceful—and sometimes not too peaceful—revolution against embedded customs.

Are we progressing toward peace among the major powers? Some assert that the world has never been closer to complete annihilation. That very fact may be encouraging to realistic people, because today in an all-out war no nation could win. The very terror and doomsday that modern science is ready to unleash is the greatest deterrent to war in the history of man. There will be limited conflicts supported by one or another nation, revolution, but little chance for another world war; in fact, another such war is impossible unless nations decide to commit suicide. Modern societies with their dynamics of progress are more creative and aggressive for self-improvement than at any time in the past two centuries. Today, while competing for the goodwill of Third World nations, the highly industrial countries are competing in outer space, in the oceans, and in the sky. Mankind in spite of its rivalry in ideologies talks much about peace and listens to the complaints in the United Nations Assembly. Each country makes known its wants and needs. Foreign aid is pouring from the older and more industrialized countries to the less fortunate and emerging nations.

The areas listed above could be considered as part of our bless-

ings, knowing that we must continue to work in many other areas
to improve the remaining conditions that shout for correction. To
struggle for the betterment of mankind is the lot of the realist and
the person who realizes that striving for achievement is characteristic
of the emotionally alive individual.

Personal Changes

The program of amelioration, which has already occurred or
promises to be enlarged, has dealt mainly with the outside world.
We must now deal with your own inner drive and those of other
people toward greater self-realization and fulfillment.

What can be done to make it easier to live with yourself and
avoid the temptation to escape from your environment and problems, to be on a friendlier basis with others and thus have a better
chance to attain a happier life?

The following suggestions are touched upon only briefly here,
because we shall elaborate on them in the following chapters.

You need a reasonable conscience, one that does not make you
miserable when guilt is not justified. If your conscience is so rigid
that you cannot evaluate and discriminate because somebody else
has implanted that inflexibility, it is time for you to think over
standards that are definitely your own. Perhaps the scale of values
by which you automatically measure your conduct should be examined in terms of modern knowledge. Your code of conduct should
be geared to the approach of enlightened psychology rather than
dominated by people who are too zealous in imposing their outworn
or fanatic ideas. Wide reading, the study of social sciences, and an
honest, fearless examination of your beliefs will in many cases reveal that there is need to change some of your basic moral values.

You will be happier with yourself if you learn to love and to be
loved. Real affection in your interpersonal relationships should be
sought. Learn to be friendly, without fear of expressing affection,
with a natural comradeship, with sincerity and lack of affectation.
Love can be invited by a willingness to help, to encourage, and to
express appreciation. You will thus avoid loneliness by developing

a habit of being a good companion. As you acquire the habit of reaching out to others, you must not forget to love yourself. As has been pointed out, you are incapable of love if you have a poor image of yourself. Pick out your strong points—everybody has some—and be proud of your assets.

Our technological advances increasingly provide leisure time. It is advisable for you to cultivate interests that will enable you to enjoy your own company to avoid boredom. Hobbies will make it possible for you to express yourself constructively. You need not be only a passive spectator glued to a television set; more desirable is your ability to be an active participant.

It is also desirable that you acquire a realistic sense of values, particularly as it affects your ideas of success and failure. You will be inclined to question the conventional idea of success. Your primary goal should be contentment, with monetary reward and worldly possessions secondary in importance. This is not a recommendation that you should shun financial gain and the material things; it rather suggests that worldly gain will not bring peace of mind or happiness if the inner self is troubled and unfulfilled psychologically.

Failure is so abhorrent as a possibility that some timid souls do not venture into new challenges. You should understand that most people who are considered successful have failed at some time in their lives. If you are able to learn from your failures, you have a better chance of not repeating the same mistakes. It is sad, but although you may do your very best, have planned carefully, worked hard, prepared yourself well, you may still fail. You may as well face the fact that the Horatio Alger myth does not always work out. Luck, timing, and an adventurous spirit are factors in success. Be realistic about success and failure; what counts most is your self-concept and the will to achieve as the main drive that will bring self-contentment.

This attitude implies a sane philosophy of life. The person who has his feet planted solidly on the ground is not a square. He is rather an individual who has a firm foundation from which to fly to greater heights. A sane philosophy is not a stodgy one. It is the base from which he starts toward a morality firmly linked to his needs.

That philosophy demands that he understand the nature of the world, that he live in terms of goals worthy of his strength and talents, respecting the dignity of people and meanwhile being hopeful of the future. Your task is to achieve happiness. That is a lifetime project that ends only when your days on this earth come to an end. It is a personal and a social mixture, with many vicissitudes, sorrows, and hardships but with an equal number of triumphs. You will never, if you be wise, want to escape from it, because the adventures and the challenges are too great and too rewarding.

To know a person in the sense that you understand the bases for his faults and accept him as human being like yourself can probably be more effective in avoiding war than any antinuclear treaty.

During World War II some Americans imagined Japanese people as subhuman. They were depicted in the mass media as ruthlessly killing babies, raping women, and to inflicting unimaginable cruelty on the battlefield.

Today the younger generation, who have been spared the propaganda of a war machine, find these same people friendly, enthusiastic, and gentle as they gather on our college campuses or visit our homes. It seems impossible that only a few years ago citizens could hold such venomous hatred of another nation.

Certainly, friendship and understanding between nations are two of the most effective devices to promote world peace.

CHAPTER VII

Psychological Development

The achievement of maturity is the goal of life. But what is maturity; how can it be encouraged? How can it be hindered and prevented from developing to its full potential?

Every person has a past that can explain his present personality. Many studies have shown that there is a gradual schedule that can be analyzed to show how one's personality has evolved. Steps to maturation in a person's sexuality, for example, were traced by Sigmund Freud, the founder of psychoanalysis. Although this schema has been challenged by some psychiatrists, nevertheless it is interesting to examine Freud's point of view—leaving judgment of its validity to your own evaluation.

First, according to Freud, there is self-love; second, love for the parent of the opposite sex; third, love for someone of one's own sex; and fourth, love of a mate. The sequence is a gradual process beginning with oneself and ending with the ultimate attachment to another person that biologically sets the stage for reproduction.

The earliest stage sees the baby in love with himself, taken up with his own body, experiencing delight in mouth and lips during feeding, and in fact in the feeling of his whole body, including the genitals—although erotic sensations have not yet been centered in the genitals. At this stage of self-love, the baby may play with his genitals, which may alarm some parents. If undue alarm results from this practice, the infant may have implanted deep in his subconscious that any pleasure derived from bodily contact is wrong and sinful, laying the foundation for an unrealistic conscience.

However, the infant's greatest pleasure is now of an oral nature; great satisfaction is derived from lips, mouth, and tongue. He sucks with gusto on a breast, on his thumbs, and on any object that he can bring to his mouth. In adult years that craving partially remains in normal persons as a desire to put "thumbs" in their mouths, such as the chewing of gum, cigarette smoking, or chronic coffee drinking.

The next development in this self-love stage is the emergence of fascination with the child's own feces. Because he values his evacuation so highly, he uses it not only for pleasure but also as a means of rebellion against his mother. He goes to the bathroom as a reward both for himself and for his mother, who is often puzzled by her child's stubbornness. Because of the tendency for the child to consider his feces as valuable and to play with his excrement, parents should provide substitutes such as clay, sand, mud, and finger paints to sublimate this early inclination. Freud stresses that the way in which toilet training is handled may have a profound effect later in the personality.

The second step in sexual development involves the transformation of self-love into love for the parent of the opposite sex; the little girl loves her father and the little boy loves his mother. Later this love, if it is not disturbed by unwholesome conditions in the home, will be transferred to a loved one of the opposite sex. During this first stage of the child's sexual development, he will have many questions, such as wanting to know where babies come from and why the father has a penis and the mother lacks one. During this period, generally between ages three and six, parents have the opportunity to develop in their offspring a healthy attitude toward sex. The fact that many people fail in this period is evident in the numbers of the mentally ill whose sexual concepts and practices have gone awry.

Generally interest in sex diminishes after six years of age. Perhaps the loss of sensuous love for a time at that age may be due to guilt aroused when the inquisitiveness about babies is repulsed, by the realization that boys and girls differ anatomically, and by the secrecy about the parents' sexuality. All of these may combine to make the child shy away from the subject.

The third stage in sexual development involves the child's identifying with his own sex. This has been called a period of homosexuality, when the youngster gets a crush on his teacher, a camp counselor, or one of his peers. Since currently homosexuality among adults is not infrequent, much research remains to be done in order to find out why a man or woman becomes fixated at this stage of sexuality. Freud looked upon homosexuality as the result of early seduction, poor sex education, or segregation in prisons or the armed forces, emphasizing that homosexuality- has its roots in strained parent-child relationships. The American Psychiatric Association now considers homosexuality an illness only when it involves conflicts and guilt.

A fourth stage is reached as a teenager or slightly earlier when the normal person acquires interest in the opposite sex. The mature and emotionally healthy person finds an outlet for his sexual needs through dating and finally accepting a more or less lasting relationship upon which he can bestow his drive on a socially acceptable level, and one that will yield him his goal of happiness.

Some Aspects of Emotional Maturity

In Chapter I we considered briefly what is involved in being a mature person. Nearly everybody admits that signs of immaturity include wishful thinking, holding grudges, being too aware of other people's opinions, undue worrying, rigidity, self-consciousness, intense feelings of inferiority, and a clinging overdependency. The normal well-adjusted person, on the contrary, gets along well with others while retaining a feeling of self-worth. He sets reasonable objectives based on reality; he is discriminating as to what is important in his life; and he certainly is eager to get the most out of his existence.

A Healthy Mind

An emotionally healthy person can make his own decisions. He does not automatically reject tradition, nor does he entirely depend on it. He is not hesitant about changing his mind when new conditions or evidence seem to favor a change of course.

The mature person should be convinced that the world does not exist solely for his own benefit. Until the realization comes that an individual matters little in the scheme of things, he cannot understand how important he is to himself. To think that he has only to pray and thus influence God's decision is to believe the world to be entirely in his favor. Leaning on God in some instances is based upon the feeling that life owes us things for which we are unwilling to work. Many religious leaders today favor greater maturity in our concept of God.

Worry plagues the immature person. Realizing that it is not the way to deal with difficulties, the worrier goes over his problem again and again in vain. He merely repeats negative and emotional responses, regretting a past that he cannot change.

The emotionally healthy person, on the contrary, proceeds in more sensible ways. He accepts the fact that his anxiety may cloud his view of the future, knowing that perhaps his fears magnify the problems involved. He sits down to clarify and to examine the difficulty in a clearer light. Once he has done this, generally he discovers that the situation is not as ominous as he thought it to be.

Now he sets a definite time when he can concentrate on the problem. Then he considers possible solutions, weighing each in turn. He resigns himself to the fact that the best solution may not be practicable; then he decides on pragmatic courses without tension. Finally he may realize that a cure for his worry may be in reeducating himself toward a more mature personality.

Control of Feelings

The ability to withstand tension and strain is one of the marks of the emotionally stable person. Consequently he has enough control not to react too quickly to difficulties or opposition that may arise. He learns to evaluate situations with calmness, objectivity, and deliberation. He can accept criticism without being hurt if he deems it justified, and he has managed not to be dominated by childish fears. The controlled person has outgrown blind obedience and adolescent rebellion. Those people who are always ready to participate in demonstrations or riots—not knowing exactly why—are frequently those who have not outgrown the adolescent tendency to be against anything that seems to offer an opportunity to express continuing subconscious hostility against their own parents.

Both radicals and those of the extreme right have failed to resolve early and childhood fixations; they are still trying to free themselves from vested interests presumably held by school, church, and other authority substitutes. That tendency does not necessarily mean that anyone who wants to change society is immature. It does imply, however, that he who is still fighting his parents may actually not be interested in human betterment, but merely be concerned with rebellion. The progressive who wants to improve his lot and that of mankind is engaged in a crusade, possessing advantages for fellow-human beings.

Social Adjustment

Social maturity is indicated when a person neither depends on his family nor fights against them. He has attained security in friendships. He has handled his sexuality in a manner that does not create problems. He accepts some customs and conventions as a means of obtaining order and safety. Generally he knows that some of his liberties must be curtailed for the good of society as a whole.

Morality

Many of our moral codes are based on nebulous ideas—particularly among young people. The older generations base their codes largely on practicality, answering the question: Does it work? These pragmatic people assume that something is good if it works and bad if it doesn't. However, one's scale of values is often based on habits and experience. Despite this, morality should evolve from training and experience; it should not be entirely imposed by authority figures, but should emerge from within oneself to meet one's needs without harm to others.

Your morality must be your own regardless of its source or origin. That responsibility is yours; it must emerge from the core of yourself to yield peace instead of guilt and fear—while still being endowed with tolerance for those who differ in their moral views.

Measures of Maturity

For many years we have been measuring intelligence in the sense that we can predict success in schoolwork and the ability to learn. The score is a measure of a person's ability to progress at a given pace, termed an intelligence quotient, or I.Q. Benet, an academic psychologist, learned through research that a person can accomplish specific tasks of increasing difficulty as he grows up to adulthood. Physical development can also be measured according to established scales.

But now we are not concerned with intelligence or normal physical development. We are considering emotional maturity in itself without denying that there may be positive correlation with other measurements. Psychologists have ways of ascertaining progress in emotional maturity from infancy to adulthood. However, the testing in other areas is much more advanced than the measuring of emotional adjustment. This may be because not all social scientists agree as to what is maturity in emotional development. In any case, the discussion in this book definitely refers to emotional health as shown in social independence, self-help, communication, self-direction, appropriate vocation, and pleasant socialization. As the person grows in emotional maturity, he expects social freedom and reaches for an ever-widening circle of friends and agreeable associates.

Fixation and Regression

Many obstacles mark the process of becoming emotionally mature. Thus there occur fixations, the tendency at some point to remain unchanged, and sometimes there are regressions to earlier stages of development. An example of fixation is given by the chronic alcoholic who remains in the oral stage, like an infant who can be satisfied only by having something in his mouth. An example of regression is provided by a person's going back to an earlier stage of development under stress that he cannot handle on the adult level: the person, for example, who throws a temper tantrum characteristic of the infant in the process of toilet training.

Our progress toward emotional stability is hampered by two personality conflicts: the urge to grow opposed by a desire to go back to infancy, to have someone pamper us, assume our responsibilities. The urge to grow up, to stop being a child, to become a part of society is normal for any given age. It involves courage and the stamina to take risks, the willingness to give up some privileges and to take on the obligations of a normal adult.

Some people are afraid to assume responsibility. They may have a nervous breakdown when asked to accept a bigger job. Anyone can regress to childish behavior when he feels compelled to assume stress too heavy for his ability to adjust.

Although in most of us there is an irresistible desire to grow, nevertheless hindrances, hardships, and disappointments, particularly the sense of being rejected, may stop our normal progress toward emotional maturity. A child is easily discouraged. Barriers limiting development are generally created by parents and teachers.

Barriers are created when children are too confined in their activities, when they are largely limited in self-expression, when too many "don'ts" are imposed. In this manner, we mold a world that is too harsh for the child and too punitive, with resultant confusion and neurosis.

Fixation, as already mentioned, is the arrest of psychological development at an early stage of growth. We say that a person is fixated when he does not continue to grow emotionally beyond a certain point. He is stuck somewhere along the line of progress, remaining too long in a childish state. The reasons for such a stoppage are varied, but the principal one is believed to be excessive dependence upon the mother. Overprotection of a growing child, a smothering love, is sometimes worse than no love at all.

A mother whose love for her son is overwhelming, often replacing the love once held for her husband, boasts about her adolescent offspring, sharing all his secrets, impulsively pushing him toward specific educational programs, approving or disapproving his dates. She may end up with a highly educated professional man—but one who has remained fixated to his mother's love. No other woman can please him. He will either remain single or marry someone who reminds him of his mother. He may fail in all his relationships with women as well as in his work, because he has never been able to develop self-responsibility.

Other signs of fixation may be identified as follows:

Boasting. It is characteristic of childish fixation when a person has to boast in order to assert a hoped-for superiority. Bragging about one's achievements, material possessions, or appearance reveals a sense of inferiority. Some people spend their lives trying to impress their friends, never reaching a sense of well-being because they remain like the little boy who announces that "My father can lick your father." Strutting like a rooster over beers in a tavern, such a man may be meek and submissive at home.

Bullying. Picking on weaker people is a mark of the fixated person who has failed to develop a sense of worth in his early years. Whether it be physical abuse or sarcasm, it is a childish way of seeking to prove one's superiority.

Temper Tantrums. The spoiled child stamps his feet, cries until he seems about to choke, perhaps rolls on the floor, yelling. An adult may likewise express uncontrolled anger, hoping to get his own way, fighting at the drop of a hat—especially if he is tackling a smaller man.

Negativism. The sulking, stubborn spirit displays the rebelliousness of a four-year-old child. Such a person is against everything. The world is going to hell, and anyone in a position of authority is automatically a crook or a rascal. War is inevitable, and mankind should be blown to hell.

Putting Off. The habit of postponing important assignments or duties is a sign of childishness. A letter is never written, home work is neglected until the last possible moment. Such stalling is a habit that reveals a person as fixated to the irresponsible child.

Self-indulgence. Excessive pampering of self is a form of infantilism. Such people cannot deny themselves immediate satisfaction. They buy on credit without thinking of the ability to pay later. Luxuries come first even though there is hardly enough to eat in the house. If there is a choice between a bottle of liquor and paying a medical bill, the extravagance comes first. Even bestowing expensive gifts that one can ill afford is an overanxious effort to buy affection or love.

Crude Humor. Broad humor such as custard-pie comedy in movies and on television appeals to puerile laughter and entertains the immature person. Equally childish are practical jokes such as pulling a chair from under a person about to sit down. Such ideas of humor may be appreciated among young children, but rarely by the more emotionally mature.

Living in the Past

Looking to the past rather than living in the present is a form of regression. Middle-aged or older people who talk of old times and magnify past exploits often deceive themselves. The so-called golden days of yore are largely fictitious and an attempt to withdraw from the here and now. Regression in a harmless form occurs when grown men attend conventions where pranks and practical jokes abound.

Pathological regression is generally present in those who are seriously ill mentally, living in a childish world of sorrow or in the omnipotent stage when wishing was deemed the magic through which all desires were fulfilled.

What are the causes of regression? Why do people return to a previous stage of development?

Severe frustrations may lead an emotionally weak person to regress to what he once considered a safe condition. A woman, for example, will return to her parents when her marriage is on the rocks, going back home where as a child she found security and moral support.

The essential motive for regression is the inability to mature, a desire for a less complicated way of reacting. Regression is giving up on adult reality. A form of regression in this country is shown by people who prefer to watch television rather than engage in conversation, read good books, or participate in physical activities.

Regression often occurs during illness. The rugged and masculine man suddenly begins to make childish demands, reacting in a surly and unreasonable manner—as is often discovered by nurses, doctors, and wives.

CHAPTER VIII

Early Experiences

Psychological growth is like a ladder that must be climbed. If you ascend one rung at a time according to what is normal, you will ultimately reach as high as your potentialities warrant. If through unfavorable circumstances you look down as you climb and actually go down instead of going up, you are regressing. If you stop at a given point, you are fixated at that level of your development. If, however, you continue going up, looking particularly at each rung at hand while occasionally glancing upward to the challenges still ahead and planned, you are progressing satisfactorily, with a resultant sense of achievement and well-being.

The way you start this climb and the circumstances surrounding this beginning of your life are extremely important for your future. Accordingly, we shall examine infancy to see how you may have been influenced negatively or positively during these early years. You will see yourself in some of the subjects discussed. But you need not worry if you recall that things could have been better in your family. The important factor at this point is self-understanding, the insight that will enable you to acquire greater emotional health today and tomorrow. We speak of the past at this point not as a form of regression but as a means of self-improvement in the present.

Psychological research has consistently indicated that the mother is the most important influence in the molding of an infant's personality. If all mothers were free of neurotic traits and were emotionally mature, the chances for improving mental health in the next generation would be tremendously enhanced. Any observer of child-rearing sees ample evidence that instinct is not enough to guarantee a mentally healthy youngster. The modern woman generally knows that to provide ideal conditions for her infant requires that she become familiar with the psychological factors that favor a healthier development for her child.

Even under the best of circumstances, an infant becomes anxious when he feels insecure. For that reason, psychologists advise that a baby up to 18 months of age should not be separated from his mother for a whole day unless a grandmother or another person who has been close to the infant remains with him. A baby who has not had the opportunity to establish empathy with another person is apt to be anxious and fearful of being abandoned when away from the mother.

Unheeded crying, delayed feeding, chastisement, shouts, and threats all tend to arouse anxiety in the baby. Inconsistency is also anxiety-producing. Being indulgent at times and arbitrarily punitive at others is conducive to insecurity, conveying the idea to the infant that the world is unpredictable and often cruel.

Love is as important as an adequate diet. The feeling of belonging as part of the family is essential for establishing a sense of security. The baby needs repeated evidence that he is loved. Having received much affection, later on he will tend to be friendly, accepting even strangers as persons with whom he can feel safe. With this assurance of being loved, the infant is well on his way to establishing social relationships with other members of the family and the community outside the home. It has often been observed that good citizens, good mates, and good parents are generally from homes where love was freely bestowed upon growing children.

Much research has been done to prove that mothering develops the infant's personality. The baby should be caressed frequently, not only when the mother feels like it. It must be emphasized that a baby is not strong enough psychologically to tolerate privations. Consequently he should be held and fondled when he cries and fed when he is hungry. Otherwise his tension and fear of abandonment are increased. Bathing should be a pleasant and soothing experience for both mother and infant, instead of being a chore.

Scientists have been impressed by the unusual stability of the people of Okinawa. In spite of the hardships of tropical diseases and the ravages of World War II, they were found to have few mental ailments. It was discovered that they were rarely psychotic or afflicted with psychosomatic symptoms, and crime was practically nonexistent among them. How could these Okinawans on their Pacific island maintain their emotional health in sharp contrast to the people of Western civilization?

The answer was believed to be in the way infants were treated. First of all, the baby was breast-fed until at least two years of age. During that period the mother rarely left the infant. She carried him on her back wherever she went, working in the fields with the baby strapped close to her own body. Whenever he showed signs of hunger, he was simply shifted to her breast where he fed until satisfied. This way of life tended to instill the confidence that mothering was always there for the asking, preventing a warping of emotional development.

The infant has a feeling that the mother is a part of himself, that she is in fact his ability to get what he wants. If she fails to provide a sense that the world is good and giving, she disrupts this inner feeling of power and the infant receives a serious blow. The consequences may be the early development of neurotic trends that could carry over into adult life. If this early insecurity is severe enough, the infant may remain fixated to his mother in such a way that he remains a mama's boy, incapable of making normal adjustments to other females.

The brand of mothering in Okinawa does not produce spoiled brats. Rather these children are cooperative and responsible, having self-reliance and the confidence that nothing harmful can come to them. Evidently the easy-going ways, the pampering of infants enable them later to live in harmony and social cooperation, strong enough to withstand psychic stress without falling prey to emotional illness.

In our culture infants are too frequently emotionally warped by a feeling that they might be abandoned. This shock and others already discussed arouse anxiety before the youngster is strong enough to withstand it. These experiences are not integrated in the infant's consciousness because the nervous system is not yet mature enough to record the memory. The trauma are therefore imbedded in the subconscious. They can be brought to the surface by psychoanalytical techniques when the adult is plagued by neurosis of which he has little conscious understanding.

An aspect of Okinawan family life is a permissive attitude toward children. The child is not forced to do anything upon demand. In fact, there is no bowel training. At about three years of age the youngster learns from his peers—when he is ready of his own free will—because he is then strong enough for self-control. Respect for the child's personality is basic in that culture.

The contrast between our demanding and often punitive society and theirs is phenomenal. We not only control, but we threaten and very often spank. In contrast to Okinawan culture, ours is typically disrespectful of the child's personality. It is perhaps little wonder that the strong hand of authority is so often demanded to run our world, that periodically dictators have their appeal when difficult social upheavals are upon us.

Parents therefore should not be afraid to shower love on their offspring because of a fear that they will spoil them. The mother who really loves her infant will be ready to attend to his needs, knowing that it is important for the baby to be gratified and that deprivation in these early years can be definitely harmful.

Many studies of so-called spoiled children reveal the same sequence of strict adherence to rigid training and a strange belief that too much affection is bad for a child. Few children are spoiled by too much love if at the same time they learn to be self-reliant. The term self-reliance should be imprinted in our minds, because permissiveness without self-responsibility is disastrous.

Many psychologists have praised the Okinawans, stressing the permissiveness of their society. Accordingly, it has been implied that children should be allowed to run wild, with their aggressive and destructive tendencies freely expressed. These psychologists, mainly of some decades ago, had conveniently forgotten the second half of Okinawan training, namely that of self-reliance. The consequences of a lack of self-reliance are almost terrifying, involving destruction of property, crime, and scrawling of graffiti.

Graffiti, for example, is even held by some to be an art form. If graffiti is an art, so is digging a hole in the ground and urinating in it, because both are forms of expression originally motivated by a need. Permissiveness is not enough, particularly if it be preceded by infantile years filled with frustration and bad mothering.

The Okinawan youngster is taught responsibility by the general atmosphere in his society and by the examples of his peers. Permissiveness is only half the lesson; and leaving out the second half, responsibility, has been the curse of modern education and of our system of justice.

Some mothers in fact do not know the necessity of balancing love with initiative in their offspring. This "smothering" is exemplified by a woman who not only dresses her 13-year-old daughter but also punishes her by sending her to bed in the afternoon. Another still cuts her child's meat at meal times. The desire is not to develop self-reliance but to perpetuate infancy long past the first few years of life. Other instances are the mother who accompanies the youngster to and from school even though the distance is short, and the mother who sleeps with her son beyond the eighth year. Later these mothers will use their "sacrifices" as evidence of their love and devotion to create guilt in the son or daughter—little realizing that by those very practices they have arrested the development of the child for whom they proclaimed love. The permissiveness that such a mother bestowed on her child provided him with everything he wanted except the security that can come only with self-reliance and responsibility.

Certainly it should be stressed that in infancy the baby should get what he needs and wants. However, as he becomes stronger and more aware of his environment the time must come in the child's development when there is wisdom in making demands, either by parents or by the culture, denying what is unreasonable to encourage him to do for himself what he is able to do.

The spoiled child exhibits selfishness and impudence. He is a nuisance in the classroom, being totally unprepared for social relationships and the demands of a world where his babyish whims will no longer be forgiven.

If we emphasize being spoiled by the mother, it is because her influence is much greater with the infant. However we could also mention "Pop-ism," the tendency of a doting father to grant his offspring every wish when the child has reached the stage when self-reliance should be encouraged.

Anxiety by Proxy

The insecure mother fears that something bad will happen to the child unless she takes the utmost precautions against any possibility of accident or harm. Unfortunately her fears are conveyed to her offspring. The overanxious mother finds it difficult to relax. She is ever on the alert for symptoms of illnesses, and if the youngster does become sick her anxiety is aggravated. Because the infant's world is so dominated by his mother, the anxiety and insecurity are absorbed by the infant as if by osmosis.

Projected Hostility

Pampering of the child is often the result of overcompensation by the mother. Feeling hostility, conscious or subconscious, toward the child, she feels guilty and seeks to offset that guilt by leaning over backward in bestowing favors and attention. The father who feels that he cannot provide adequate affection for the child may similarly heap toys and other material things on him to soothe his own conscience. Such pseudo-love does not deceive the child; somehow he feels neglected and betrayed while at the same vaguely disturbed by a feeling of guilt because he cannot love his parents in spite of all the attention he is getting.

The Unhappy Home

The mother who is disappointed in her husband and lives amid a sullen and bitter atmosphere in the home often seeks consolation in her child. She clings to him, directing all her frustrated love to him. However, the child actually feels that he is bearing the brunt of an unsatisfied love life and tends in the end to reflect the mother's bitterness.

Parental Rejection

If overprotection is harmful, rejection by parents is equally devastating to the child's emotional growth. Delinquent children are nearly always rejected children or through various circumstances feel rejected. Those children who feel unloved become restless, nervous, ever seeking attention through making trouble at school, vandalism, or crime. The problem has been widely studied, and the conclusions always indicate that emotional starvation is the primary cause of criminality in young people. Emotional disorders in the home provided an atmosphere conducive to antisocial behavior. Again and again researchers have found that juvenile delinquents have been deprived of a close relationship with the mother and have had their infantile need for love denied.

A feeling of rejection may not even be based on fact. If the child is made to feel insecure through discord in the home, he may well imagine that he is not wanted. With an inclination to question his parents' devotion, the child thus filled with uncertainty may look for evidence of rejection. Unfavorable comparison with someone else, more attention to a brother or sister, being called stupid and yelled at in desperation can combine to enforce the child's suspicion that he is not wanted.

The traditional concept that all women love their children is a myth. Some mothers hate their children because they never wanted to have them in the first place. Overheard complaints about being tied down, about slaving for the children's upkeep and education may indeed convince children that not only are they a burden, but also despised. These expressions of hostility made in moments of frustration are disastrous to children whose ego strength is not sufficiently firm to withstand such attacks on their personalities.

The child must have love and affection even when his conduct is unsatisfactory. The parent who punishes a child calling him a bad little boy is attacking his basic security. On the other hand, if the parent emphasizes that the punishment is given, not because he is unloved, but rather because such conduct is unacceptable, the child can understand. If the child feels that he will be rejected when his behavior is bad, he is in fact being coerced into good behavior in exchange for affection. On the contrary, if love is freely bestowed regardless of behavior, punishment is seen as a nonreward that can be tolerated because his parents' devotion is still assured.

In American culture, in contrast with a less strenuous pattern in other societies, parents push their children into a mad pursuit of success, with the implication that failure will automatically bring rejection on the part of the parents. Our children are subject to great emotional strain when there is the threat of rejection if they fail in school or in subsequent lifework.

At the beginning of the Russian Communist revolution 24-hour nurseries were introduced, on the premise that the state could do a better job of rearing children than the family. After some years, however, the idea was discarded, because children away from their parents failed to acquire a normal amount of aggression and lacked a sense of independence. With the family reinstituted, Russian soldiers fought aggressively, with great courage in defending their homeland. The link with their native villages and cities was strengthened because it was connected with the loved ones awaiting them upon their return.

Babies raised in institutions in this country are similarly deprived of emotional support. For that reason, children left with welfare agencies are placed with foster parents as soon as possible. If the choice of such foster parents has been wise, children receive the fondling and love that they crave, with resultant good adjustments.

Eating Problems

Feeding problems particularly in the first two years of life account for many disturbances among children. The idea that the baby must be kept to a definite schedule may actually cause malnutrition by emotional upsets in both the baby and the mother. Deceived by the notion that she knows the nutritional needs more than he does, she

forces the child to eat. Her approach is authoritative and demanding: The boy will grow into a big boy if she has to kill him to do so.
Emotional reactions are evoked by such treatment. Unfortunately,
the more conscientious the mother is, the more she insists, and often
she has an infant who refuses to eat and spits out the food. If only
the mother realized that the baby should be fed when hungry instead of according to an arbitrary schedule.

The child cries and whimpers for food, but this kind of mother
pays no attention. It does not matter that the child is ready to eat,
that his little stomach is not geared to an artificial schedule. He
screams. Nothing happens. As a result he becomes anxious. The
world has abandoned him. To the baby the world is now, with no
yesterdays or tomorrows. When his appeals bring no response, he
feels rejected. With repeated experiences of this sort, the mere sign
of hunger will arouse anxiety, and the mother has laid the foundation for oral problems in adulthood that spread to situations far
removed from the routine of eating.

Patterns are set when the infant is delayed in the gratification
of hunger. You have met some grown persons who become un-
reasonably angry when a meal is not on time or restaurant service
is slow. Many adults cannot put off gratification. They must have
what they want immediately and are highly annoyed if their wishes
are denied. These people perpetually live their infant anxiety when
their hunger was not relieved. They had to wait under extreme
frustration, and in adulthood they refuse to be denied because such
deprivation merely reactivates a hunger long passed.

An opposite pattern may be set by early postponement when the
infant is not strong enough to withstand the frustration. This pattern involves the infant's learning to bear an enforced schedule. He
learns to suffer in order ultimately to satisfy his hunger or desire.
This ability to postpone pleasure to the future is generally desirable
as a trait of a healthy person. However, infancy is too early to
acquire this habit. Instead of developing a desirable trait at this
stage, it engenders a masochistic tendency that invites suffering.

For a person who has been conditioned to accept suffering as a
means of attaining gratification, success can come only through great

sacrifice. Such a person feels guilty if accomplishment occurs without effort. Happiness is reached only through self-denial. He tends to be an ascetic who feels guilty if he allows himself a good time.

A third pattern developed from early eating frustration is the pessimistic attitude caused when the crying infant was finally convinced that no matter what he did, it was of no avail. This type of person was disillusioned in infancy. He expects nothing and is cynical because his personality was molded when his crying was of no avail. The mother, having denied him what he considered love in being fed, engendered insecurity. The world was indeed cruel, and finally he gave up, expecting no response to his crying. Thus later he assumed that there would be no reponse to whatever he might demand.

Still another pattern may be set during infancy. Suppose the mother decides that the child has been fed enough even though he is still hungry. This pattern, if repeated often, produces a person always wanting more than he has been given, a trend that is prevalent in our competitive society. Should we blame the economic system or the mother? There is evidence supporting the assumption that the denial of infantile needs does lead in many instances to insatiable avarice.

The Bathroom

Freudian psychoanalysts have stressed the influence of toilet training as most important in shaping personality. Regardless of disagreement among professionals, common sense indicates that the formation of toilet habits is the source of parent-child animosity.

It is true that the emotional stress involved in the process of toilet training is trying. This is especially so if the mother forces bowel control before the child is ready. The demands of cleanliness are frequently given priority over the child's need to progress at his own pace. The mother should be aware of the fact that the youngster's muscles are not strong enough to control his eliminative function until about eighteen months after birth.

The real harm of too early toilet training is the adverse effect on the child's feeling for other people. The threats often made by the mother arouse rebellion and negativism, accompanied in the youngster's mind with anxiety and insecurity. Punishment connected with failure to control evacuation may easily become associated with the genitals, complicating later sex life with disgust and aversion. Personality is certainly influenced by what takes place in the bathroom between mother and child.

A baby is born the most helpless of creatures. He cannot talk, walk, or take care of himself. Were he not immediately sustained, death would come within a short time. And in comparison with other species he remains much longer dependent upon others.

Before birth, the neonate is nestled warmly in the womb, well-fed, and absorbing peace without effort. The process of birth, on the other hand, is one of pain, a rude awakening to the harshness of the outside world. The howl of the newborn could therefore be one of anger at the loss of a cozy nest where there has been neither stress nor conflicts.

Apart from genetic factors, this small infant will now be at the mercy of other people. Their ignorance can damn him to neuroticism or to the challenge of living a life full of wonder and achievement.

CHAPTER IX

Childhood Years

The indulgence recommended for the infant should gradually be shifted to the training of the child for reality. This process includes the gradual introduction of some frustration, discipline, and concern for the rights of others. Although permissiveness is essential in the infantile years, it must be lessened as the child grows older. Modern educators often stress the need for developing the independence of the child. But more frequently it is forgotten that without self-discipline and the ability to get along with others, the person cannot gain independence except in the sense of being an outcast from society, turning that society against himself, with resultant loneliness if not bitterness and resentment.

The child-centered school or home seems to have few rights for elders. Parents or teachers are beginning to realize that it is unwise to sacrifice too much for the sake of satisfying the whims of the child. It is a mistake for parents to deny themselves the meeting of their own needs in order that their children may have luxuries. Youngsters who are thus pampered do not learn to respect the rights of others. Hardships in a family should be shared by all its members. The attitude thus engendered for achieving common objectives makes for emotional growth in children. The essential training at the childhood level is that which encourages socialization, concern for the rights of others, and self-reliance.

At about the age of three the child is confronted with demands to establish relationships with other people. His selfishness is challenged by the expectations of others, although he is pulled by the desire to be a person in his own right. At this point he may become confused and respond with hostile refusal. This is a time of resistance that may take the form of regressing to bedwetting, renewal of eating problems, and other forms of hostility.

79

Later, as we shall see in the next chapter, there will be another period of negativism in adolescence, when the urge to become independent again rears itself. Meanwhile, the child of about three years has to make some kind of adjustment.

Standing Still

The child may decide to remain at his present stage of development. He refuses to take further steps as if saying, "So far and no farther." No matter how the mother seeks to induce him to do new things, the child resists. He will not get on a swing like other children, nor will he learn to eat like grownups. If taken to a carnival, while other children squeal with delight he is totally indifferent. Sometimes parents may begin to suspect that the child is mentally retarded, whereas actually he is merely difficult—sometimes as a result of earlier mistakes of upbringing during the infant stage.

Regression

In other instances, as already noted, there occurs a regression in the child's behavior, a return to conduct that was appropriate to an infant. Perhaps he felt more secure as a baby, and under the stress of socialization and getting used to other people he returns to his infantile ways. A mother becomes concerned: The child whines and cries, and his toilet habits regress to babyhood. The indication here is not so much to worry that the child is not progressing, but rather to question the relentlessness with which he is being pushed or has been asked to assume conduct for which he is not ready. It should be emphasized that although there are norms by which the child's emotional and physical growth may be measured, nevertheless each child is different and should be allowed development uniquely his own.

The Quiet Child

Because of anxieties caused by stress at the age of two or three, the youngster may become introverted; that is, he may turn away from reality because it is too demanding. If treats or punishments are used to make the child more civilized, he may console himself by thumb-sucking or masturbation. This latter habit may alarm parents; instead of forbidding it, however, the wiser course is to distract the child into more satisfying activities with toys or praise for achieving something else. Making him feel bad about his own body and the fact that he seeks security through erotic touching of his genitals can only create a foundation for guilt in later sexual activities.

The Rebel

This is the difficult child who "drives mothers crazy." They throw up their hands in near despair, exclaiming, "I just don't know what to do. He's impossible!" There is constant spiteful rebellion and sloppy eating and elimination habits. The child seeks to destroy everything he can get his hands on. He throws stones at other children, abuses the dog or cat, and stages violent temper tantrums.

We have already discussed the mistaken treatment of infants that in turn pays such negative dividends as these. Fortunately, when the youngster reaches the age of five he will have outgrown his contrariness. By that time, he will have a firmer concept of himself and will have the wisdom to accept the authority of adults.

Obedience

The most important way of obtaining obedience is to give commands only when they are essential and then, with rare exceptions, insist on their being carried out. If the parent is consistent in this practice, the child soon gets the idea that he must obey. There are, of course, parents who issue orders merely to enhance their own desire to dominate. A father may have little authority on his job, and he may seek to compensate by bossing at home. Under such circumstances the child soon becomes aware of this unreasonableness and seeks to rebel against it.

If consistent discipline is imposed, stress should be shifted to self-discipline. However, some overanxious parents are afraid to aim in that direction lest the child get into difficulties. The more emotionally balanced parents will, on the other hand, allow their offspring to take the consequences of his actions, thus developing self-responsibility. The goal of wise discipline is to eliminate it. One should not take these recommendations as suggesting that the parent should suddenly decide to do nothing to guide the child. The parent should always be ready with advice and guidance, but decision should ultimately be left to the child whenever possible.

The Sick Child

Emotional difficulties can evolve out of a child's illness because of the wrong way in which he is treated. How should a sick child be handled? This is a question that harasses parents, because anxiety is generally a part of the situation.

Most of the nursing falls upon the mother. The child wants more attention than usual and frequently judges the seriousness of his ailment largely by the mother's reactions. The bedside manner should be calm and reassuring, even though under certain circumstances it is difficult to maintain such stability. Anxiety and tension in the mother may make the child respond in a similar manner, creating the possibility of exacerbating the illness.

Overprotection and oversolicitude during a lengthy confinement may create an infantile neurosis of extreme dependency, with the child perceiving an apparent reward of greater attention while he is ill. Later as an adult he may retain a tendency to be a hypochondriac because childhood illness paid off in increased solicitude and what he construed as love.

When a child is sick in bed, it is best not to display any apprehension. The mother should speak in a normal voice, calmly, no matter how she feels. The youngster must recover from his sickness not only physically sound, but also psychologically unhurt. Part of the goal here is to prevent complete dependency on the mother, with a consequent loss of self-confidence and acquisition of an inferiority complex. The mother should be careful not to imply that it is more fun to be sick than to be well. If the child has always been treated with love and affection, the added attention demanded by his sickness will not seem unusual.

Surgery can have a traumatic effect unless proper preparation is made to avoid undue fear in the child. Psychologists recommend that the youngster be told what is to be done. The mother can also arrange to be with the child before and after the operation. The surgeon should not discuss the case within hearing of the patient, nor should any instrument be visible to arouse fright.

Jealousy

When mother comes back from the hospital with another child, jealousy may appear. Thereafter for many months she must devote most of her time to the new baby. The other child feels neglected, and if he is not overtly hostile he may hide his true feelings with apparent solicitude for the baby. It takes a wise mother to show that she loves the new sibling with equal tenderness, explaining his helplessness in comparison with her bigger boy or girl.

Another type that can prove even more devastating is that of being jealous of a parent—the parent of the same sex of a given child. If the son loves his mother and feels that she loves his father, he may suffer pangs of jealousy. He wishes to keep his mother all to himself. If the daughter loves her father and he gives evidence of love for the mother, the girl child feels jealous, wanting to keep her father's love exclusively hers.

This triangle occurs when the child is five or six years old. It is the cornerstone of classical psychoanalysis. The resolution of the trauma connected with this jealousy and its complications is central to a psychoanalytic theory.

The Freudian approach has been cited in an earlier chapter. Whether or not one agrees with it is secondary in this discussion. However, it has often been observed that a little boy will push his father away when the father seeks to kiss his wife; and the little girl will similarly want to prevent her mother from embracing the father. This tendency toward rivalry and jealousy in the child may account for the fact that witnessing sexual intercourse between parents can be a traumatic experience for a child.

Giants and Dragons

There has been criticism of the amount of crime and violence in the mass media. The very people who have been raised on Grimm's Fairy Tales, Shakespeare, and the Bible—three of the greatest horror sources—express concern about the influence of movies and television on their offspring. Every kind of sexual perversion has been described in the Bible. Shakespeare's plays depict the widest variety of deceit and man's inhumanity to man; and Grimm's Fairy Tales drip with blood, murder, and cannibalism. This literature has been a part of the culture, the intellectual nourishment of the most sophisticated, often the kindest of human beings. Even erotic appeal is far from absent in our most appreciated art. Here we immediately get into an argument between appeal to puerile interests and that which is lifted to the artistic level simply because someone says it is art. A nude is a nude whether it is displayed in a museum or on the cover of a magazine; in fact, the statue is considered to approach perfection to the extent that it most nearly duplicates the human body—beautiful or ugly.

But before getting into an argument with art critics, let us examine the reality of the influence that fairy tales have upon our children.

Sexual Curiosity

It must be realized that children have a natural interest in sex and violence. An urge to see the difference between male and female is present in early life. The need to examine and to solve the mystery of the human body is an important part of the child's imagination. Frustration of this need when it is condemned as wicked and dirty implants in the youngster's mind the belief that sex and erotic feelings toward one's anatomy and that of others must intrinsically be wrong and wicked. The result of this prudery is the basis of many neuroses. People may sublimate such a neurosis, of course, by becoming artists obsessed with the nude or by choosing medicine to satisfy an insatiable desire to peer into human conditions ordinarily hidden from others. Even the scientist whose curiosity leads ever into the unknown may subconsciously be seeking the solution that he failed to find as a child when he was barred from solving the mystery of the opposite sex. Although such sublimation can produce good for the human race, it is still true that the mark of what is falsely branded evil in the child's mind may later prevent him from achieving emotional stability.

The answer is to have honest, frank, and wholesome sex education both in the home and in the school in order to rid the child of any neurotic feelings and guilt about the human body. The problem of pornography would thus be eliminated, since both the child and the adult would no longer find it interesting. To the emotionally healthy person an X-rated movie may temporarily be amusing, but soon it becomes artificial and boring; its main attraction for both young and old is that it carries the label of forbidden.

Urge to Violence

Whenever there is excessive frustration accompanied by anxiety, it is the nature of the human being to become angry. This tendency is instinctive; otherwise the species would have died out a million years ago. Man had to fight a hostile environment or perish. Imbedded deep in the psyche of a new life is this will to live, to battle against frustration, and the infant has to begin that fight all over again. In fact, the principal task of the parent is to civilize her offspring by shifting the child's anger into socially acceptable channels.

From the very beginning tremendous frustrations are imposed on the child. The mistake is the assumption that a child is a little angel. The fact is that he is a little savage; if he had his own way he would destroy every obstacle in his path. The essential realization is that violence is as natural to a child as breathing and eating. The real problem is that of training the child to appreciate reward and love when he acts acceptably and to deny reward when his conduct is antisocial.

Our civilization exists largely because violence is controlled and directed into one's self-improvement and for the benefit of one's fellow human beings. However, when the urge to violence is not expressed positively for the survival of our culture, it is turned against society in the form of crime and inhumanity to man. If the hostility aroused by merely living in an organized and to some extent regimented society is channeled neither into acceptable behavior nor into antisocial acts, then that hostility is turned inward to create character disorders and mental illness.

The answer, naturally, is not to stifle hostility in the child, but to train him in the direction of socially acceptable expression of that hostility. Aggression can be directed to toys, to helping others, and to allowing him to overcome obstacles that he himself can remove. In this manner he can be made aware that being angry in itself is not bad. Allowing the child to get what he wants by means of temper tantrums is to steer the child toward unacceptable and destructive behavior. The ability to handle one's hostility in a healthful manner, without purposely hurting others, is the core of an emotionally well-adjusted person.

Escape from the Humdrum

To escape from reality as a general way of life has been pointed out as the chief characteristic of mental illness. However, it would be a mistake to assume that one should not seek temporary escapes from the humdrum of existence. There is music to enjoy, poetry to be appreciated, books to be read, occasional periods of solitude— and even daydreaming in moderation. The child, too, may need to escape from a nagging mother, the same routine at school, homework, and the boredom when there is really nothing to do. Fairy tales and the Cinderella type of story seem to make dreams come true and enlarge one's horizon into new wonders.

Stimulating Imagination

The more richly one's mental life is stimulated by make-believe, the more that richness will be transferred to daily life. Reading about the wondrous exploits of heroes makes a person contemplate his own potentialities, thus giving the child hope that he may in some way contribute to his own society when he grows up. Without the wonders of adventure, fairy tales, and the marvelous achievements of television heroes there would be less incentive to an appreciation of one's imagination.

Aggression in Fantasy

Childhood must learn how to handle the anger that is generally not allowed full expression. It has been stated as a result of considerable research that such repression of anger often results in absorbing the anger into oneself, turning it into insecurity and self-hate.

Many psychologists have pointed out that reading about violence and viewing fights and open aggression can act as a catharsis to draw such emotions away from the child's inner self. He expresses vicariously the anger that frustrations arouse and thus acts out the anger harmlessly. How else can we express the popularity with adults of professional boxing, wrestling, and even bullfighting or cockfighting. The Olympic Games are promoted on the premise that it is better to compete in sports than to slaughter in warfare. In either case aggression is expressed, the first in a harmless manner, the second in murder and the destruction of nations.

Contraindications

The argument that reading fairy tales and other stories of violence is an effective means of overcoming boredom is denied by people who claim that this sort of escape is far from being healthful. There must be better ways to lessen the humdrum of a child's life than witches and dragons and wolves that eat defenseless children, they say.

As for such stories stimulating the imagination, it is counterargued that the claim is spurious because real life stories of a more wholesome nature can do just as much if not more to stimulate the imagination. As for the value of fairy tales as a catharsis, it is stressed that there is already too much violence in our society. The problem, it is asserted, is to eliminate hostility and anger as much as possible, not to express it even vicariously.

The problem of television programs, movies, and other media portraying violence and sex must be approached from different directions depending on one's point of view. The opposing sides are arrayed one against the other. You as an individual will have to make up your own mind and judge for yourself whether or not you have been harmed psychologically by your early contact with stories, tales, and pictures considered objectionable by many organizations.

The childhood years largely determine the kind of future awaiting the adult. And a very simple formula operates in encouraging a mentally healthy person or one who is beset by emotional disorders.

It may seem naive to accept a formula of behavior that guarantees the maturing of a comparatively healthy human being while avoiding the development of a severely neurotic person. Yet the formula is simple enough. The difficulty is that it is so hard to apply given the complexity of those bringing up a child.

In any case, it is easy to understand that the child is subject to two forces: positive force, which is *approval*, and negative force, which is *disapproval*. If the child in the process of growing up receives more approval from adults than disapproval, he will tend to become emotionally healthy. If, on the other hand, he is the recipient of more disapproval than approval, he will tend toward being emotionally handicapped.

CHAPTER X

Teenage Stress

The time has come for outgrowing childhood; the adolescent has come into puberty, the stage of sexual awakening when the girl has begun to menstruate and the boy's testicles have produced spermatozoa. Both are now physically capable of reproduction. It is during the teenage years that sexual desires are most intense, and yet our culture still places many psychological and sociological obstacles to the expression of that sexuality. Accordingly, it is a time of great stress for the adolescent.

Many studies have been made of the culture of Samoa showing that young people there display practically none of the stress and difficulties suffered by American teenagers. In the United States youngsters are taught either directly or by implication to engage in sexual activities only after marriage has sanctified the relationship. Although that norm has been gradually and silently changed somewhat in recent years, there still remains a tendency to look askance at sexual activities.

The Samoan engages in sexual relations as soon as puberty is reached. His personal contacts with the opposite sex are casual even in marriage. There is no deep attachment. If a couple does not get along they simply separate, each to go his or her own way. The children are no more disturbed, simply moving in with friends or relatives.

American teenagers are burdened by too many decisions to be made as to careers, further education, affiliation with different institutions, political leanings, religion, and a host of others that tend to arouse anxiety and conflicts. In Samoa there are none of these; the youngsters simply live without regard to the past or future.

Some of the most difficult problems of his whole lifetime must be made by the teenager at a time when he is least qualified by experience and least prepared to deal with them. There are four areas of emotional conflicts in the trying and stormy years of adolescence.

The Need to Be an Individual

The young person wants to find himself, to become an individual whom he can call his own. In seeming contradiction to this desire is the urge to be one of a group, to be gregarious. Teenagers love to congregate in clubs, community centers uncluttered by adults, and even on street corners—not to mention organized gangs. In these areas of gregariousness, young people tend to be extreme conformists, wearing identical jackets and emblems as a sign of belonging, talking alike, and even thinking alike. At the same time the adolescent is struggling to be a person in his own right. The severity of the conflict thus emerging can be highly disturbing.

The manner in which this dilemma is resolved depends largely how the teenager has been treated in infancy and childhood. Children who have had normal opportunities in growth and development will be able to go through adolescence with comparative ease. They can look forward to adulthood with little distress. The adolescent who can live without any great denial of himself and of others is well on the course of mature adult adjustment and peace of mind.

The Need for Confidence

The fight for confidence by young people is opposed by an underlying uncertainty. They do not feel sure of themselves, partly because of their newly awakened sexuality. In many other areas they question previous assumptions and possibly their basic faith.

The doubts are part of new emotional vistas, a demand for evidence, a questioning of authority, a desire for explanation. They are a groping for a different way of life, a philosophy to follow in an obscured future.

During this period, the young person is very sensitive to criticism or disparaging remarks. He needs much support at home to offset the challenges as well as the defeats that confront him at school and among his associates. Every effort should be made to uncover and promote his talents in order to give him greater opportunities and a sense of achievement. Parents should understand that the bravado and bragging of the young person are a form of compensation for his sense of insecurity. Praise at home should be expressed liberally no matter how he is regarded elsewhere. Building his self-confidence is vital at this time. Parents who understand this need in their growing boy or girl will help in any way possible to boost his or her morale and self-assurance.

Emancipation

Leaving home emotionally, liberating himself from family dependence, is a difficult adjustment for the young person. It is not easy even when the home has provided a favorable climate, and it is extremely hard if the parents have been overprotective.

Signs of this struggle for emancipation are secretiveness, a none-of-your-business attitude, a determination to do as he pleases, to have his own thoughts, and sometimes open rebelliousness.

The wise parents will accept this disturbing way of life in their offspring, neither approving nor disapproving, only hoping that the rebel of today will in this manner work his way to well-adjusted adulthood.

To belittle parents is part of growing up. This may be done by the youngster by looking down on the father's profession or criticizing the mother's taste in clothes or hairdo. When direct attack is too threatening, the adolescent may use an indirect approach. For example, the son of fastidious parents may show his rebellion by appearing dirty and careless in dress to show that parental teachings about cleanliness and order have been in vain. The current fashion of disheveled hair and patched Levis—copied by many adults—seems to be a national and even an international fashion to show disdain for authorities and the establishment. Young people will no doubt continue to change their styles later as they become more predisposed toward innovations as part of their desire to be different.

The quest for emancipation is progressing when a youngster refuses to disclose his or her plans for the evening, when the boy no longer wants his father as a pal, when lack of cooperation becomes evident. Certainly parents have a problem on their hands as their offspring goes through the normal routine of establishing himself as an individual with responsibilities and independence of his own. Wise parents will feel consoled that the youngster is on his way to a healthy adulthood.

Sexual Needs

A most serious problem for the adolescent concerns his sexuality and how that need may be met. Our society, although more permissive in recent years, still imposes taboos against premarital sex and masturbation—largely supported by some churches and legal sanctions. However, many research projects have revealed that this societal opposition is not generally being followed in actual practice. It has been stated, perhaps facetiously, that 99 percent of males have masturbated and the other 1 percent lie about it. In any case surveys have shown that more than 90 percent of males have engaged at one time or other in the practice. Sooner or later the adolescent discovers that an impressive number of his peers do not seriously accede to the view of some elders.

Even most physicians today see no harm in masturbation as an outlet for sexual tension until such time as an acceptable relationship can be established with a member of the opposite sex. On the other hand, it must be realized that the practice can be psychologically harmful if it is accompanied by shame and guilt. Today's adolescent generally feels that he should progress to the heterosexual experience with a mate similarly inclined.

Venereal disease and pregnancy apparently are not sufficiently feared to deter many from satisfying their need for sexual intercourse. Accordingly, more teenagers are being advised to use contraceptives, although the rate of illegitimacy seems to indicate that such protective measures are frequently overlooked. It is evident to many social workers and psychologists that virginity and chastity are not widely accepted by today's teenagers.

The sex drive is so powerful and so persistent that it generally must find an outlet in a variety of ways. Among these are nocturnal emissions, masturbation, heterosexual petting, premarital relations, marital intercourse, extramarital affairs, visiting prostitutes, homosexuality, and other less common practices. The point to be emphasized is that the peak of the sex drive occurs in adolescence, at a time when the law, many religious groups, schools, and other institutions frown on sex activities. Whether one approves or disapproves of this code of morality, it must be acknowledged that sex is a matter of frequent conflicts and maladjustment in young people.

Some psychologists have offered the opinion that petting is a way of learning how to express and to receive affection, a preliminary and innocent approach to love-making. On the contrary, genito-urologists assert that indiscriminate fondling can be harmful because the excitement and tension aroused are not consummated with actual intercourse. For both young people petting may turn out to be a sexual fraud because of unsatisfied desires; the sex urge remains blocked and physiological shock results, they say.

To the author of this book, a psychologist treating emotional disorders for some twenty years, the assumption that heavy petting tends to cause psychological and physical harm is false and sounds very much like the old story that masturbation was the cause of insanity and other nonsense concerning sex. Although sex education is not part of the training of medical doctors, younger members of that profession generally have rid themselves of such sexual myths and fallacies. In my own experience in treating young people, I have yet to find a case in which petting has proved detrimental. It is a fact that petting does create tensions; however, those who indulge—if not released by actual intercourse—usually find an outlet through mutual masturbation or by themselves. Nocturnal emission, or having an orgasm during sleep, is another harmless occurrence that is nature's way of providing release of tension created by fantasies, petting, and other sexually arousing situations.

In European countries during past generations, the teenager was frequently advised even by his own father to patronize a prostitute as part of his growing up. In this way, it was thought, his sexual needs would be satisfied while awaiting a more acceptable mate. Although this motive rarely applies in our culture, young men are not always against the practice of seeking out a prostitute who demands neither emotional involvement nor the preliminaries of dating. However, there are hazards in such a premarital practice, whether it be in a paid-for union or with the promiscuous girl next door. Under such circumstances, a person may feel disgust along with the release of his tension. Sex for both boys and girls may thus acquire a connotation of vulgarity. Particularly for the girl who wants merely to experiment, the act may prove a disappointment and lead to the conclusion that the pleasure connected with the act has been exaggerated. Respect for the other person seems to be a prerequisite for full sexual satisfaction.

Illicit affairs often lose their attractiveness because of the necessity for concealment. Love in the back seat of a car may give temporary satisfaction to the man, but the woman is apt to derive little pleasure if intercourse is hurried and surreptitious. More lengthy signs of respect and affection are elements valued by a woman before she can give herself completely to erotic desires. Many husbands who seek the help of marriage counselors have yet to discover that a woman wants romance, love gifts, and appreciation of her person before she can be effectively aroused.

Another possible hazard in premarital sexual intercourse fortunately can be avoided if the drawbacks are guarded against. The girl may use sex merely to attract or hold a man. Employing sex purely for this purpose can lead her to neglect the development of more fundamental assets of her personal charms. The male, on the other hand, can thus overvalue the physical aspects of love, hindering his ability to feel love as a deep psychological aspect of his growth. This outcome is more likely if he is ever on the prowl for a girl who will readily yield to his advances. Using sex for one momentary thrill after another, without emotional attachment, usually conditions a person toward superficial social relationships.

The average teenager needs above all else a feeling of security and self-worth found in real affection, the knowledge that his sexual needs can be satisfied without sacrificing his self-respect. The adolescent can indeed profit from sound sex education that will provide him with scientific, physiological, psychological, and ethical knowledge. Through such education divorced from prudery and hypocrisy, he should be allowed to get the information that he needs to guide him in these areas. Such guidance, however, must not be in the form of authoritative dicta. It must be related to the world as it exists for young people, not as it is conceived to be by their elders who often are impelled by out-of-date orthodoxy.

The controversy about sex education in the schools continues unabated. If sex is deemed to be dirty, then the subject has no place in the curriculum. If, however, sex is considered to be a normal human function—in fact, the dominating force in our lives—then to leave sex education out of our schools is to deny our children a vital part of their training for healthful living.

Even those who accept the need for sex instruction disagree as to how much sex there should be in sex education—what should be left out and what should be included? Extremists argue that homosexuality, for example, should be included.

The problem is therefore to compromise between two extremes: those who want too little in the curriculum, and those who want too much. The happy medium should be the norm. Normal sex as defined by mentally healthy individuals should be our goal. Within that range, sex demands a place in our schools if children are to be prepared for a better life.

CHAPTER XI

Adult Years

The problems of adulthood are many, and they will be handled satisfactorily to the extent that the course of life through the early years has been comparatively smooth. We are the result not only of our genes—over which we have little control—but also of our past. We have been molded by our family and society and by the nature of our reactions to these forces.

The adult may decide to remain single and arrange his life accordingly; but generally the problems of the adult are to reach a satisfactory adjustment to marriage, to set up a home with the right atmosphere to raise children, and to support his dependents by succeeding in a career. The woman has the further choice of making a career or remaining a happy homemaker.

There are many obstacles in seeking these goals. Monogamy is often hard to maintain, rearing children wisely is a difficult task, getting along on the job and becoming active in the community are all challenges that frequently are arduous. Far from solving problems, marriage compounds them. Marriage brings out defects in personality and conflicts that often lead to the divorce court.

Psychologists and marriage counselors can testify that sexual adjustment is the central objective of a happy union. As the problems of married life accumulate, one of the partners may seek to escape from the pressure through extramarital affairs. Authoritative sources assert that about half of married men actually engage in sex outside of marriage. Of course, the hangups and the drawbacks of earlier patterns of sex tend to be repeated in the married state. For example, if a female has been extremely inhibited in her teen years, she may find it difficult to lose that inhibition in marriage. Some 40 percent of women are frigid at one time or other, and some are never able to achieve orgasm. The man also may prove to be unsatisfactory.

Apart from the fact that one or the other of the partners may be not responsive enough, other factors invite straying from marriage vows. A mate may feel a need for variety, someone new to stimulate waning sex desires. Extracurricular attraction and philandering complicate life, compelling the straying mate to lie, to invent stories, and to twist and distort married life. Financing such escapades may at times be difficult to maintain or explain.

Most adults manage the responsibilities of married life. The mates manage to adjust. The most trying time may be a greater readjustment after children are added to the family. There are then severe stresses when the mother must frequently remain cooped up in the home with energetic and mischievous youngsters, while the father must increasingly keep his nose to the grindstone on the job to feed his brood and to make ends meet.

Disillusion and even despair can come when illness occurs, bills accumulate, and the cynicism of disappointments creeps in with worries and frustrated ambitions.

Creative persons often reach their peak around forty. During those years, men generally are attempting to prove themselves, and married women share vicariously their husband's progress. If the woman also has a career, her satisfaction may double. It is the age of climbing the ladder of success in our system of private enterprise.

We have examined many of the obstacles standing in the way of achieving emotional maturity at the various stages of growing up. This was done not so much to educate young people as to provide information by which insight may be acquired for greater understanding of the self. This type of reflection is generally necessary for self-improvement. In the next chapters, we shall continue to be specific, fostering a greater awareness in coping with emotions.

Meanwhile, starting now, you can begin to widen your consciousness of your environment, reaching out for new goals, new challenges, and achievements worthy of progressive and satisfying adult years.

CHAPTER XII

Living in a Troubled World

The emotional stress in our society seems to be increasing. Many among us are in trouble emotionally. Some sociologists assert that Western culture is sick. They point out the vast technological innovations in which many people feel estranged, having lost the art of neighborliness. The teeming cities are riddled with crime and a ruthlessness that alarms those who are concerned with human values.

The statement that our society is sick implies that many people are frustrated and confused. Their personalities are twisted and out of gear with a culture that so often disregards human needs. There are many cynics, people with warped values, and discouraged citizens among us.

Psychologists and other social scientists see various areas of conflicts and inadequacies in our way of living. They point out that most of these categories are of our own making. We could have the will to remake our social patterns. We could help people toward better emotional health.

Rugged Individualism

It was emphasized that part of growing up entails the development of one's individuality, learning to be oneself and not a mere reflection of parental authority. We are speaking not of self-responsibility with proper concern for the rights of others. We are referring to cutthroat competition and the harm it inflicts on those who are less ruthless. The cost of competition at any price is responsible for the crushing of the human spirit, a sense of failure in the more honest, a substitution of hate for love.

These psychological scars are overlooked by those who admire the tough guy who has seemingly won the struggle for prestige, money, and power. Yet achievement gained at the expense of less hard-boiled people generally brings a sense of guilt that is often expiated by philanthropy. That guilt may also be projected on others in a form of anger; then the persons who have been the exploiters seek to destroy their competitors.

The exploiters in our society who impose defective and unwholesome products on consumers are often the children who were deprived of love in their growing years. It would be a mistake to assume that this is true in each case because the very climate of our culture regards competition as ordained by acceptance and approval. Nevertheless the person who makes good in a grand style, braggingly showing off his wealth, may indeed be the result of emotional deprivation and great insecurity.

The anxiety that this pattern generates calls for more effort to surpass others, giving rise to hostility against those who stand in the way. Sooner or later many people in this condition suffer a sense of failure because of their exaggerated desire for superiority, which never seems to be fully satisfied. The tragedy is that this type of destructive competition permeates the core of our society, inducing much frustration and defeat.

The Family in Trouble

It has repeatedly been demonstrated that a child has a vital need for a home where love and affection are freely bestowed. Parents also need this feeling of stability. Unfortunately our high divorce rate indicates that many homes fail to achieve this atmosphere of well-being. The increasing disintegration of family life seems to be a sign of a sick society.

Parents suffering from mutual distrust and hostility are serious threats to a child's security, subjecting him to more than usual anxieties and accompanying fears of the future. A home permeated with discord will influence the child when he becomes an adult causing him to have negative attitudes toward marriage and perhaps to repeat all over again the conditions under which he grew up.

Our cities are crowded with ghetto housing, not fit for human habitation, with too close quarters to provide privacy and breathing space. Many of these homes are headed by women harboring illegitimate broods, with no men to assume responsibility. Having a baby is often viewed not as a means of bringing a loved one into the world, but as a device for obtaining additional welfare.

Women who work outside the home may find that they cannot care for their children adequately. Promiscuity or sexual frustration contribute to difficult marriages. Young people working toward emotional maturity are not much helped by these family inadequacies. However, understanding the unwholesome conditions under which they grew up, they can extricate themselves by seeking to become more mature.

Two Discordant Elements

Prejudice and discrimination are twin scourges in our midst. These two discordant elements are particularly disruptive because it is difficult to overlook the fact that groups of the population are more prone to crime because of their poverty and alienation from the mainstream of basic American ideals.

Unfortunately hatred of less adjusted minorities tends to poison the minds of those who point the finger of accusation. Prejudice and discrimination have been called a social neurosis operating as a grave menace to people at all socioeconomic levels. Persecution of minorities is said to be a state of mind that essentially gives vent to hostility reflected from one's own self-hate. Certainly if the less fortunate people in our society are to be helped to rise above their sad existence or even their differences, there must be patience by those who are more favored. American history gives ample evidence that minorities tend to change antisocial trends into socially well-adjusted citizenship as they increasingly reap rewards of the system.

Wars

It is a rare year when somewhere on the globe a war is not going on. The United States has fought three wars in this century, winning two of them—if the term "winning" can be applied to the nation deemed to be victorious. The countries against whom we fought are now our friends. Some of our former allies are now our enemies. Shall we fight another world war to exchange friends and enemies? The fact is that our young people will hesitate in the future to fight a war that they consider unjust.

Wars are fast becoming a concept equivalent to mental illness. When a nation or group of nations have too long been denied both their psychological and physical needs, the response is frequently a psychotic anger that explodes as a catharsis to make them submit once more to their unchanged hardships. Nuclear devices are now scattered on land, at sea, and in the air, awaiting only a frustrated and desperate humanity to let loose a madness without end.

To be killed with a neutron bomb, to be made to disappear in a nuclear holocaust may be no more painful than to die from a rifle shot. Nevertheless there is the horror of millions being annihilated within a few moments, cities suddenly disappearing, leaders being as confused as children amid clouds of deadly radiation. The tension of our society is based largely on this machination of science in creating the possibility of killing off the whole human race.

The answer must be found in being our brothers' keeper, in helping our people and those of all lands toward a meeting of their needs. A society is just as healthy as the total of its members. Young people have the opportunity for self-improvement not only as an aim for their own welfare, but as a beginning toward a better fate for all people.

Moral Values

Our fast-changing moral values create much confusion and uncertainty. We are witnessing new ways of life with which we cope only with difficulty, blazing new trails while knowing only vaguely where they lead.

The traditional way of life includes getting married, having children, acquiring a home, gaining a satisfactory job, achieving some dignity in the community, and sharing in some religious faith. This series of concepts has long been sanctioned by church and state. Young people as they reached adulthood grew up in a ready-made way of life. Although they often rebelled against their elders, finally they accepted their fate and settled down in this social scheme.

The tradition of this cultural system still exists, although it is largely based on long past conditions when technology had not yet changed our world. The socioeconomic situation has been radically altered. Young people are frequently frustrated in their effort to conform to the old patterns, yet they often become confused and anxious as they seek to follow different modes of conduct. This conflict seems to be at the core of difficulties in family life.

Established religion and old beliefs are sometimes discarded; fewer young people attend church today. Religious faith is not entirely consonant with science and at times not emotionally satisfying. Uncertainty can be fertile soil for the emergence of acute anxieties. And yet this tendency to reject the old spiritual values has resulted in the apparent contradiction of a host of cults and far-out idealistic movements.

Insecurity aroused by the fast-changing trends in our midst also brings out much destructiveness and disregard for private property. Young people are not without anger in their anxieties because God appears to have deserted them and they have yet to find another God to replace Him. Nevertheless, young people living in a democracy must redirect their efforts toward more creative objectives and a better way of life for all people. A suitable scale of values to fulfill their needs will evolve in a society where emotional maturity can offset the mechanizing of existence.

CHAPTER XIII

World of Psychotherapy

Where does a person go if his personality is seriously disturbed, if his emotions are beyond coping with? Who are the professionals qualified to help? Who are the quacks in the field of psychotherapy, and how can you tell one from another? What do you do if you can't afford the fees of a licensed professional?

Let us first list the various types of psychotherapists, examine the general qualification of each, and note who is licensed and who is not, including the many quacks awaiting the unwary and the uninformed.

The Psychiatrist

This is a physician who has been trained in medicine followed by postgraduate studies in psychiatry and an internship, generally in a mental institution. However, the law does not prevent the average doctor with only a meager knowledge of psychology from treating the mentally ill. For that reason, anyone seeking psychotherapy from a physician should make sure that the person from whom he seeks help has passed the State Examining Board examination specifically for psychiatrists and has served an internship in an acceptable psychiatric center. Just as many physicians practice surgery without having taken the extensive training for that specialty, so some physicians offer psychological services without the arduous course of study necessary to become a specialist in that area.

In recent years a trend has emerged for psychiatrists to use a vast array of drugs, which have replaced previous medical procedures that had proved largely ineffective. As a result there has been a tremendous decrease in the number of inmates in mental institutions.

With the increased use of drugs, patients are returned to outside communities, where they are sufficiently tranquilized to exist in a sort of stupor, uncured generally, but subdued enough to live without physical harm to themselves or other people. Although this trend has saved considerably in tax money, the question increasingly asked is whether or not the removal of the controlled and protected environment of institutions creates greater insecurity for both patient and community. There are few studies to determine the side effects of such massive use of drugs, but some people in the world of psychiatry are skeptical. However, for the psychotic who finds it difficult to respond to psychotherapy and who is far removed from reality, there are few choices but complete trust in the psychiatrist and his drug-oriented treatment.

The Psychologist in Private Practice

In practically every state psychologists who offer their services for a fee must be licensed. They must devote seven years of study in colleges and universities approved by the state, hold a doctorate in psychology, take a series of examinations set by a Board of Examiners, and then serve two years of internship in a mental institution or mental health clinic in order to be licensed. Only then are they permitted by law to open an office and charge fees for their services.

The psychologist is forbidden by law to prescribe drugs of any kind or in any way practice medicine. He certainly agrees with this decision since he knows, as does the physician, that mental illness in the overwhelming number of cases is not a medical problem. Emotional disorders are functional; that is, they are not physical, but purely in the domain of psychology. When a psychologist and a psychiatrist work together as a team, the latter handles the drugs when necessary. The psychologist then views the medication as a means of tranquilizing the patient sufficiently to make it possible to reach him through psychotherapy.

The psychologist, however, tends to limit his practice to the treatment of the various neuroses, including the phobias. The psychologist also treats psychosomatic illnesses with the close cooperation and the team approach of a physician in consultation.

About ten percent of the population—some 22 million people—are in need of psychotherapy, mainly for neurotic conditions. In some areas the problem is even greater, with some 90 percent disclosing that at one time or another they were in need of help for emotional disorders. There are not enough psychiatrists and psychologists to handle this national problem, and increasingly these two professions are joining hands to help alleviate the problems of emotional instability.

The Psychoanalyst

This specialty belongs to the physician who becomes a psychiatrist with emphasis on Sigmund Freud's theories. An increasing number of psychologists are being trained in this field, practicing particularly in large cities and suburban areas. The specialty requires at least four years of study after the physician has qualified in medicine. The psychologist also must have the same number of years of study beyond the doctorate in psychology. The lay analyst—one who has substituted psychological training for the medical—must do the same as the medical psychoanalyst. The physician spends seven years in colleges and universities to obtain his medical degree. The psychologist spends a similar number of years to obtain his doctoral degree.

Once this basic education has been acquired, both the physician and the psychologist must thereafter spend at least four more years studying the basics of psychoanalysis. Both professionals have now spent at least eleven years in their studies. In addition one must add a two- or three-year internship in a mental institution or a mental health clinic. And further in addition to all this, the psychoanalyst must undergo a period of two to four years being analyzed by another analyst to make sure that he does not carry neurotic tendencies into his work. In other words, he must prove that he is emotionally mature and free of hangups before he is allowed to practice his profession.

Ultimately the physician must pass a series of tests set by a State Board of Examiners in order to qualify for a license as a psychiatrist, and the psychologist similarly must pass his own state board exams to be licensed as a psychologist. Both psychologist and psychiatrist are now licensed and permitted to practice their profession. At this point, however, they are required by their respective professional associations to practice for some 200 hours under the supervision of an established psychoanalyst in order to avoid the mistakes of a beginner and to develop further the vast amount of knowledge acquired over the years.

A psychoanalyst generally does not depend on drugs in his treatment. Considerable changes in Freud's teaching have emerged in recent years. With a lengthy and demanding training behind them, it is to be expected that psychoanalysts' fees should be high and often beyond the reach of many people. However, some psychoanalysts—with a medical background or with one purely psychological—adjust their fees according to the ability to pay. In any case, with increasing coverage of psychological services by insurance companies, more and more people are now able to afford the fees of these highly trained professionals.

The Marriage Counselor

Several states now license this specialty. It has been in past years a lush field for quacks. However, several years ago a national organization called The American Association of Family and Marriage Counselors was formed to lessen the abuses of unqualified practitioners. Membership requires a doctoral degree in medicine, social work, or psychology with additional training in marriage counseling. In addition the practitioner must have proved his competency.

With the increasing divorce rate, and with greater expectations from marriage, it has become more common to seek the expert knowledge and techniques of these professionals. Some marriage counselors are also trained in sexology and help in sex maladjustments, a frequent problem in discordant marriages.

In most states, however, marriage counselors are neither licensed nor recognized. This means that anyone with a will to profit at the expense of turbulence can put out his shingle and charge whatever the traffic will bear. A host of people without qualifications are exploiting the public. If a couple should feel the need of a counselor to save or to improve their marriage, one of them should consult a librarian, who can determine whether a given counselor is a member of The American Association of Marriage Counselors—preferably one who is also licensed as a psychologist, social worker, or psychiatrist.

The disruptive forces of some personality trends, outside the consciousness of the parties concerned, often are the cause of marital conflict. Expanding knowledge about domestic strife is available to well-qualified counselors to enlighten unhappy couples, to avoid divorce, and to reestablish a better husband-wife relationship.

The Social Worker

Professionals in this field are trained to work, particularly for adoption agencies, on welfare problems and for clinics. They are licensed on the master's level. Although they are not licensed for private practice or for psychotherapy with the intent of collecting fees, as long as they do not call themselves psychologists or psychiatrists no law prevents them from doing so. It is expected that their efforts to persuade state legislatures to license them for private practice may yet succeed. Meanwhile, next to the licensed psychologist in private practice and the psychiatrist who is Board certified, the social worker is in a position to provide satisfactory services for his clients.

The School Psychologist

This specialist is trained to work with children in school, with teachers, and with parents. Training includes the master's degree and frequently includes courses beyond that level. An increasing number of school psychologists have acquired the doctoral degree. Beyond that point, they may have passed the tests and met other requirements for private practice. Some of the better-qualified school psychologists remain in the schools while engaging in private practice in their spare time; they are allowed to charge fees for their services because they have completed the mandated training and have become fully qualified to treat patients outside the schools.

Yet those whose training limits them to practicing school psychology at a salary paid by a school district are a very important part of the mental health team. It has been stressed throughout this book how influential are the childhood years in developing personality. A school psychologist should be employed for every 300 pupils in the school not only to offset the stress put upon the child during these years, but also in order to understand the pupil, to motivate him properly, to guide him toward the achievement of emotional maturity, and finally to make smoother the task of learning.

The school psychologist serves an essential task of helping teachers and parents toward a better grasp of the child's problems and suggesting how to solve them. The school psychologist is a friend and a sympathetic listener, because he himself has generally reached a high level of emotional maturity. The easiest way to consult a school psychologist is to go directly to his office and request an appointment. A parent can find the school psychologist serving his child by calling an administrator in the system and asking for psychological advice concerning a given child.

The Guidance Counselor

Children in the school need guidance in subject selection, preparation for a career, and college choice and admission. Although these areas are the primary concern of the guidance counselor, he also complements the work of the school psychologist in helping the child to grow emotionally. The psychologist in the school system gives tests and evaluates them and guides teachers toward the improvement of the child's academic progress and development.

The guidance counselor, working with teachers and school psychologists, helps to create respect for each student as a person in his own right. One of the aims is to stimulate success within the reach and capability of each child. At the same time, this specialist tries to provide conditions conducive to better instruction in the classroom, recommending avoidance of sarcasm, blame, and other practices that work unfavorably on the pupil's personality.

Guidance counselors can be reached in the same manner as school psychologists. Both these disciplines can contribute much to young people's emotional growth.

The Clergy

Some training in psychology and counseling is now included in preparation for the ministry. Priests and rabbis are also increasingly informed concerning symptoms of mental illness. Of course the typical seminary courses offered do not qualify the clergy for licensing as psychologists.

The clergyman nevertheless is asked for help by members of his congregation, praying with the man who has lost his job, commiserating when a family member dies or divorce is contemplated and when quarrels arise with children or relatives. The minister, priest, and rabbi all offer premarital counseling. It is their responsibility to enrich the spirituality of their congregations, to give them a message of hope based on mutual faith and the exemplary conduct of their personal lives.

In some large churches psychiatrists and psychologists are on the staff, acting as consultants or accepting referrals to their services. Since psychologists need not be licensed to work for an agency, the client has no assurance that he is receiving the counseling appropriate to his illness. However, some of these church-supported programs do offer real help and are especially appreciated by many with a religious background. The clergyman may thus be effective because prayers, religious faith, and some psychological studies combine to offer solace and advice to parishioners.

The Criminologist

There is much similarity between psychotherapy and the way in which criminologists view the lawbreaker. The psychologist looks to his patient's past as a key to his present behavior. The crime specialist proceeds on the same assumption. Those who are less psychologically oriented do not dispute that the experiences of childhood may have been such as to adversely affect the criminal's personality; but the penologist may presume that the only way to rehabilitate a transgressor is to punish him.

The criminologist, usually academically oriented, holds that one cannot rehabilitate a criminal without understanding his background and the basic reasons why he became antisocial.

The penologist, who tends to be oriented toward the more traditional approach, is concerned with making prisons more escape-proof and requiring the regimentation of prisoners and stricter discipline.

Both exponents, when extreme in their views, may be responsible for the failure of our system as it exists today, creating great cynicism on the part of ordinary citizens. Currently it costs as much to keep a person in jail for one year as it does to support a family of four for the same length of time.

Judging from the increase in crime, there is little rehabilitation, and the fact that criminals rotate in and out of jail. seems to be ample reason to question the wisdom of those who set the tone of our prison system.

Perhaps the main cause of failure in handling criminals is similar to the failure of our educational system to develop a majority of students who are emotionally mature.

It was pointed out when discussing the factors that influence childhood growth of personality that permissiveness is necessary under certain circumstances, but that at some points self-responsibility must be developed—sometimes involving suitable punishment.

Possibly the criminologist is wrong in stressing permissiveness without responsibility; and the penologist is equally wrong in stressing punishment without permissiveness. The answer possibly lies in the merging of both views, allowing a prisoner sufficient latitude to encourage self-worth and self-responsibility coupled with being ready to punish when that permissiveness is abused both for self-harm and the harm of his fellowmen.

The Counselor in Industry

The counselor in business or industry is generally a psychologist or social worker. He need not be licensed for his job, and he receives a salary; therefore he charges no fees for services rendered. He may be called an industrial-relations counselor, personnel director, motivational specialist, or other title. His main aim is to make the workers happy and as well adjusted as possible to employment, thus indirectly bringing profit to the firm.

A good job is more than making money. It is a means of expression, an opportunity to associate with people of similar interests, and a way of gaining status in a community. The personnel counselor will guide an employee toward work best suited to his skills and personality. From there on, the counselor must continue to measure the worker's ability to do his job satisfactorily.

In a large organization, an employee may feel that he is no more important than the machines or the books that he keeps and the records that he files. In order to avoid this alienation, the worker needs to have someone like the industrial counselor whom he can trust and who can be concerned for his well-being.

Some counselors view their office as a first-aid station for mental health where a disturbed employee can unburden himself without risking his job. The aim is to forestall more serious emotional difficulties. A mentally ill person is a poor investment for an employer. The daydreamer may be prone to accidents. The insecure person is upset by changes; he can disrupt the morale and efficiency of a whole group. A more humane approach to production can pay dividends not only in the worker's adjustment, but also in added production.

Although there are many advantages in consulting with an industrial counselor, particularly to advance a young person's career and to seek vocational guidance and ways of improving his work, nevertheless there are areas of serious emotional difficulties that preferably should be handled by the worker's own initiative. Making an appointment with a licensed professional outside the place of work is more suitable in drug or alcohol addiction. This assures complete privacy and the avoidance of whatever prejudice may exist in the minds of fellow-employees and associates who may hear of his difficulties. Such disclosure is rare, but in any case treatment by a psychiatrist or psychologist in private practice is apt to bring better results.

The Hypnotist

Hypnosis is being utilized increasingly by qualified psychiatrists and psychologists as a tool for the treatment of neurosis and as an instrument for removing bothersome habits or symptoms. Unfortunately it is also being used by many quacks and cult leaders. The licensed psychologist or Board-certified psychiatrist knows that the mere removal of symptoms such as alcoholism, drug addiction, headaches, and wife-beating is not the total answer to these problems. Excessive smoking, for example, may be a subconscious desire for self-destruction. When a symptom or a compulsive habit is removed it is generally replaced by anxieties and new defenses in the form of different and in some cases more serious problems.

The highly qualified professional gets at the causes of self-defeating conduct at the same time as he uses suggestion for its elimination. Instead of merely getting rid of the disorder, he employs a system called hypnotherapy or hypnoanalysis, being careful not to arouse more anxiety than the patient can bear at a given period. This "timing" is extremely important, and the ability to control it is an art that generally can be acquired only through training and experience.

Use of hypnosis for weight reduction is similarly subject to abuse and dangers. Obesity is often a reaction to lack of love or else a self-destructive course of action, a subconscious attempt to make oneself unattractive as a sex object—not to mention a symbol of despair, a giving up, and a belittling of self-worth. Merely losing weight under these circumstances when motives are hidden from the client may arouse intense anxiety that cannot be handled without professional help.

Accordingly, one should avoid hypnotists who advertise in magazines and newspapers. Contrary to popular opinion, hypnosis handled by one not a licensed or Board-certified professional can be far from harmless. Psychologists and psychiatrists do not advertise except to list their names in the classified section of the telephone directory as a convenience for clients. Anyone not licensed is forbidden by law to call himself a psychologist if he is engaged in private practice, charging for his services. If you need hypnosis as an instrument for treatment, be advised to seek out qualified people.

The Quack

Although quacks exist in the medical and other professions, the world of psychotherapy is riddled with them. Even in the most literate and affluent communities, few people are able or knowledgeable enough to distinguish between a quack and a well-qualified licensed or certified psychotherapist who has met rigid training requirements.

What is psychotherapy? Who is a psychotherapist, and how does he acquire that name? Well, psychotherapy merely signifies that a practitioner seeks to influence behavior through psychological means. There is no law against that, and pseudo-therapists take full advantage of that wide definition. Anyone can be a psychotherapist—a truck driver, a housewife, a welfare recipient. And, of course, since psychotherapy is the core of all services provided by psychiatrists, psychologists, and highly qualified personnel in the mental health field, it must be concluded that we are speaking of the training for the services rendered.

For a better understanding, for example, anyone can play baseball. But there are bad players, average players, and league players. No one prevents them from participating in the activity. There is no law against it. Similarly, anyone can be a psychotherapist. Under the law no one can prevent him from being a psychotherapist. However, there are bad ones, average, and those who have proved their capability through extensive training and passing of Board examinations, such as the psychiatrists and the psychologists.

The criterion for judging the competence of a mental health worker is simple enough: Is he licensed by the state or is he not? We are referring here to his right to call himself a psychologist, and not merely a psychotherapist, which is the prerogative of anyone regardless of his training. To call yourself a psychotherapist has no meaning except that you personally decide to assume that title. A psychologist, however, can collect fees for his work and may assume that title only after the state has certified his competence.

Psychologists, psychiatrists, and marriage counselors in those states where they are licensed operate according to standards set by their own professional associations, which are either state or national —such as the New York State Psychological Association and the American Association of Family and Marriage Counselors.

There are a host of charlatans posing as psychotherapists of various sorts, including vocational-guidance specialists, hypnotists, and consultants on personal problems. They exploit the unwary and the mentally ill. They disguise their incompetence behind impressive diplomas and associations of quacks, displaying their phony degrees while swindling the public. If their phoniness were limited to extracting millions of dollars from a gullible public, the situation would not be so severe. However, with more than 20 million people in this country needing psychotherapy, the problem of the psychological harm inflicted on these unfortunate people is stupendous.

If you have need of psychological services, look sharply at the practitioner's office wall. Is his state license for the current year on display? Such display is required by law if he calls himself a psychologist and also demands a fee for his services. The state certification in the form of a document will also be on public view. Is he a member of his state psychological association to guarantee that he will live up to ethical practices and conduct? Never accept the services of a psychotherapist without questioning him about his training and qualifications.

How do you find a qualified psychologist? The most comprehensive directory of licensed psychologists is the *National Register of Health Service Providers in Psychology.* Your library probably has a copy of this listing, or you may write to the publisher at 1200 Seventeenth Street N.W., Washington, DC 20036.

Qualified marriage professionals are listed in the *Register of the*

American Association of Marriage and Family Counselors. That directory is also available from your library, or you may write to the publisher at 225 Yale Avenue, Claremont, CA 91711.

What if you cannot afford to pay the fees of a licensed professional? Make an appointment and state your case and financial obstacles. Many psychologists and psychiatrists lower their fees in certain circumstances. On the other hand, practically all major medical insurance policies now cover 80 percent of charges for psychotherapy if the practitioner is a Board-certified and licensed psychologist or psychiatrist. For those on welfare receiving psychotherapy from such personnel, the county social welfare agency will not only pay the full fee but even provide transportation to the practitioner's office.

If none of the above sources are available, the public clinics operating on the county level offer therapy free or at a minimum charge depending on your ability to pay. However, since many of the psychotherapists practicing are beginners, charging lower fees, it might be wise to examine other referrals before committing yourself to the public clinic route.

In any case, it is wise to note that visiting a psychologist today is no more a stigma than to go to a physician's office for a physical ailment. In fact, it is a sign of maturity to seek help toward self-improvement and peace of mind.

Paradoxically, often those who are in greatest need of psychological support are the most prejudiced against consulting a mental health professional. A person who seeks a psychologist to become a better person, a happier person, is not crazy. He is merely wiser than those who belittle such help.

CHAPTER XIV

Wheel of Despair

There are more than 30 different schools of psychology from which the psychologist molds his system of treatment. It has been estimated that as many as 10,000 devices are available for use in effective psychotherapy. It can be well understood that those who have had little training are meagerly equipped to serve clients in distress.

Each psychologist, nevertheless, develops his own methods based largely upon the research of other social scientists, modifying earlier concepts, offering the treatment most appropriate to given patients. He may eliminate or change what he firmly believed in the past.

The author of this book frequently uses a schema that enables him to trace the development of a neurosis and to help alleviate it through an analysis of its position and progress.

The patient's thinking seems to follow a series of steps or cycles, rotating on the axle of a wheel. More specifically, the cycles are:

Frustration (Cycle I)

Numerous examples of frustrations have been provided in this book, tracing their frequencies from infancy to adulthood. We could have continued into middle and old age. At every level of existence there are inevitable frustrations. Some of these are physical obstacles, others are psychological. In fact, the psychological disappointments are possibly even more severe, as is evident in the fact that there were fewer mental illnesses during the bombing of London in World War II than there were in peacetime.

One cannot avoid frustration. It is a part of life. Even the tree has to fight the law of gravity in the process of drawing sap and nourishment for every limb. Our lives are a constant process of overcoming frustrating circumstances both within ourselves and in the outside world. Walking is merely a process that prevents us from falling. The way we handle frustration, or Cycle I, determines the nature of the second cycle in our psychological status.

Anxiety (Cycle II)

When frustration occurs in the satisfaction of needs and desires slight anxiety arises with unimportant and unthreatening obstacles, and extremely severe anxiety when such blocks pose a great danger to our well-being. Of course, the frustration is most serious when the person has made his way to adulthood under some of the stresses described earlier in this book.

The anxiety therefore differs in degree and intensity depending on the seriousness of the situation and the strength of personality. It may be a physical threat, as when being confronted by a mugger; or it may be psychological such as rejection by others, a situation in which a sense of self-respect is denied, an insecurity that permeates one's whole being.

Anger (Cycle III)

At the same time that anxiety is felt, anger emerges either only barely discernible, or with a deep consciousness of irritation and annoyance. When this anger wells up in the individual, his instinct tells him to act, to do something to reduce the frustration. In any case, however, he will react in one of three ways: (1) he may run away from the problem, thus assuring its continued existence to plague him; (2) he may decide to fight in the sense that he confronts the frustration—with the average person successful at this point; or (3) he may turn the anger against himself, thus setting the stage for the next cycle.

Guilt (Cycle IV)

If the anger is turned inward instead of outward, it is an admission of guilt, of a sense of unworthiness; the person blames himself for his dilemma. Or the guilt may have been aroused because he acted against those dear to him or contrary to his conscience.

The way a person handles his anger is therefore very important. Anger must be expressed one way or another. If it is expressed in a socially unacceptable way, it similarly engenders guilt.

The manner in which anger is given vent largely determines whether or not the person's conduct is emotionally mature or the opposite. If he resolves his problems, eliminates them, or neutralizes their effects, he thus turns his anger toward his environment and not against himself. He is avoiding a sense of guilt, particularly if the action is of benefit to others as well as to himself.

Guilt may impel a person to change his ways, to step out into the world, to fight the good battle, overcoming obstacles instead of being defeated by them. However, without that turnaround, guilt becomes a pernicious and destructive factor that leads to the next cycle in the development of mental illness.

Self-hatred (Cycle V)

Hatred of self is often the consequence of guilt, since that feeling is an admission of blaming oneself for the failure to solve frustrating problems. It is a corrosive feeling that eats into the personality. The person feels unloved, abandoned, on the assumption that others have reason to detest him. The possibilities that his associates may find out the real nature of his abominable self makes him still more unsure and insecure.

Here, as in the earlier cycles, the possibility always exists for turning back, taking an inventory of one's good points. You can determine no longer to duck your problems, firmly deciding to do something about them, and letting the anger be directed toward constructive avenues. Arouse yourself. You were meant to fight, not to cringe, hugging self-hate and discouragement. Life is a struggle, so get on with it, and stop the self-pity.

Depression (Cycle VI)

Self-hatred because it is so negative ultimately leads to the cycle of depression. The person seems to give up, assuming that all struggle is useless, with no possibility of happiness in any form. There is loss of interest in members of the opposite sex. Love is dead, and the person is incapable of affection. He is wrapped up in his private hell and is alone.

The loneliness is overwhelming. The feeling of rejection by the world is felt as reaching deep within the recesses of his soul. He is adrift without a cause or a sail, and all around the sky is dark—not even a storm is expected to stir up the miasma of the dead sea.

This kind of depression, when it persists for some time, generally indicates that professional help is needed. However, cases of severe depression have been overcome by a sudden change in environment, the reawakening of interests. The endless patience and understanding of people close to the mentally ill may be difficult to maintain. There are dangers of suicide during this precarious period.

Pervasive World Hatred (Cycle VII)

The depression of Cycle VI strangely sometimes seems to disappear, or possibly is repressed by the development of hatred of practically all living things, all institutions, coupled with distrust of everybody. This is a projection of one's anger outside of the self, but it is destructive.

In its extreme form the neurosis approaches the psychosis to superficial observation. However, the person is now able to function, unlike the conduct of the psychotic whose world is bizarre. Whereas the neurotic suspects that others are planning for his downfall, the psychotic hears voices and his own speech is odd and sometimes incomprehensible. The psychotic may commit murder because an imagined being tells him to do so. The neurotic at this stage may also kill but out of uncontrollable anger, meaning to inflict harm for the injustices that he imagines have been imposed upon him. Whereas the psychotic can kill with no emotion whatever, the neurotic belonging in this cycle acts in a spirit of revenge. He is totally aware of what he is doing, knowing the difference between right and wrong, unlike the psychotic whose deeds of violence have no connotation of rightness or wrongness. That is why the psychotic is confined to a mental institution and the neurotic is sent to jail when either commits a crime of violence.

What becomes of the neurotic in Cycle VII? The likelihood is that he will not turn violent enough to come into conflict with the law. However, his conduct is so obnoxious to others that they retaliate against him, repeatedly rejecting him as a trouble-making malcontent. His neighbor treats him with disdain, store clerks rebel against his bitter and continuing complaints, and he finds himself shunned by old friends. The neurotic in this cycle incurs still greater frustrations, adding to those he already possesses.

With added frustrations piled one upon the other, the seven cycles start all over, revolving on the axle from deepening anxiety and anger, which now becomes more intense. The neurotic finds himself reacting in the same way he reacted originally. The repetition of self-defeating behavior according to patterns already set is characteristic of the neurotic.

Thus this mentally ill person is caught spinning on his wheel of despair.

It is the task of the professional psychologist to stop this rotation from frustration to the hellish world of the neurotic when his illness has reached the stage of complete disillusionment and hatred. The degree of his ailment will be determined by the negative progress he has made on this wheel of despair. The psychotherapist is often successful in changing personality toward greater emotional maturity.

The person can do much for himself by analyzing his own behavior, noting particularly the manner in which he handles his anger. Many suggestions have been made in earlier chapters to help in the reduction of frustrations.

It is now up to you.

Go out and do something.

Work for self-improvement and for the enrichment of your personality and peace of mind.

Index